# CLOWN ACT OMNIBUS

## Everything you need to know about clowning plus over 200 clown stunts

## WES McVICAR

MERIWETHER PUBLISHING
COLORADO SPRINGS, COLO.

791. 33    0803878⅔

**Meriwether Publishing Ltd., Publisher**
**P.O. Box 7710**
**Colorado Springs, CO 80933**

**Editor: Arthur L. Zapel**
**Cover & inside design: Michelle Z. Gallardo**

© Copyright MCMLXXXVII Meriwether Publishing Ltd.
Printed in the United States of America
Second Edition

**Library of Congress Cataloging-in-Publication Data**

McVicar, Wes.
    Clown act omnibus.

    1. Clowning.    I. Title.
GV1828.M27    1987        791.3'3        87-42958
ISBN 0-916260-41-0

# CONTENTS

# Introduction

*"Let a clown but laugh and the whole house will giggle."*

(H.R. Haweis — 1872)

## Historical Background

The origin of the English word *clown* is uncertain, but it is thought to have come from a Scandinavian or Teutonic word for *clod,* hence a coarse or boorish fellow, a lout. Clowning goes far back into history. Traces of it appear in Greek burlesque and on the Roman stage.

In the Middle Ages, kings and nobles had their fools — court jesters who were privileged characters as long as they could amuse their masters. These were often gifted musicians, mimics, skilled dancers and acrobats, full of wit and impertinence. The pointed cap and tasseled scepter became symbols of these jesters.

On the old English stage a clown was a privileged laugh-provoker. He had no real part in the drama, but carried on his jokes and tricks, sometimes addressing himself to the delighted audience instead of confining himself to the stage action.

Shakespeare elevated the clown, giving him a speaking part, often using him as a comic relief to ease the tension in his tragedies. The gravediggers in *Hamlet* are clowns. Othello had his clown. Launcelot Gobbo was Shylock's famous clown.

In France, the Pierrot in his two-colored costume was a gay, light-hearted clown, often an accomplished dancer. Harlequin, too, was of French origin, distinguished by his black mask, shaved head and expert acrobatics.

Italy gave us Pantaloon, originally Pantaleone, of serious face and baggy trousers. From Italy, too, came the interpretation of the clown as a tragic figure, laughing while his heart was breaking. Leoncavallo's *I Pagliacci,* the popular opera, is the best example of this.

Germany gave us the painted clown face, showing no personal expression.

## Clowning as an Art

Throughout the ages, the clown has used his talents of drama, music, dance, wit, acrobatics, juggling, riding and make-up to provide laughter. His greatest skill, however, has been in the art of pantomime. Pantomime has attracted some of the world's renowned artists. Charlie Chaplin's silent films have become classics. France's Marcel Marceau delights audiences wherever he goes. Many of our comedians of stage and television rely strongly on pantomime; Joe E. Brown, Red Skelton, Jackie Gleason, Sid Caesar, Imogene Coca and Dave King are among the many who come to mind.

Clowning is a real art. It requires physical skills, dramatic ability, a firm understanding of human nature, imagination, wit and a strong sense of the comic. It uses timing, surprise, anticipation, slapstick and some-times pathos as elements in its humor.

It is said that man is the only animal that laughs. Clowns down through the ages have given the world something to laugh at — and to laugh with.

## Circus Clowning

Circus clowning is of relatively recent origin, but has become indis-pensable. What would a circus be without clowns? Clowns of the "big top," such as Emmett Kelly, are internationally famous. Such clowning makes full use of its past heritage of baggy trousers, painted faces, panto-mime and physical skills. It also relies on broad humor of the slapstick variety, with its falls, blows, knavery, mimicry and frustration. To the Pierrot and Pantaloon, America has added the Hobo, the Policeman, the Rube and other characters. Certain clown acts have become tradi-tional; others are invented as needed. Very little, however, has been available in printed form, under one cover, until this book was compiled.

## Clowning for Amateurs

Sure-fire clown acts are an integral part of any amateur circus. They have many other uses, too.

They are valuable supplements to all physical education demonstra-tions. They can provide entertainment at banquets and luncheons, ama-teur shows, play days, demonstrations, festivals, pageants, meetings. Recreation departments, youth-serving organizations and schools have not made full use of clowning in their programs.

An exception to this is the YMCA Indoor Circus or Gymnastic Dis-play. *Clown Act Omnibus* has been made possible by the author's associ-ation with his own shows and those of other leaders in the YMCA.

In some communities such as Reno, Nevada, and Vallejo, Califor-nia, businessmen have found an interesting hobby and service project in clown clubs. Members of these clubs develop clown acts and take them to children's institutions, homes for the aged, children's hospitals and other institutions as a means of bringing laughter and color into the lives of the less fortunate. This type of activity is worth exploring on a larger scale.

# About This Book

This book contains over 200 workable clown acts. Since the origin of many of them is extremely vague, it is difficult to give credit where credit is due. The author therefore thanks all in general who have carried on the circus tradition with clowns and clowning.

Even for the most inexperienced clowns many of these acts will prove sure-fire. The more difficult acts will require training. Any production, of course, is the better for good planning, preparation and rehearsal.

Though only 168 clown acts are numbered, there are many subdivisions of additional stunts which bring the total in the book to well over 200. The reader's attention is called to the fact that the Index of Clown Acts, alphabetical by title, at the end of the book, gives the *number of the act* — not the page number.

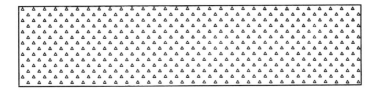

## CHAPTER 1

# A Word on Clowning

Clown acts look simple and easy. Like good tennis players, golfers or experts in other sports, clowns must be so skilled that their acts look effortless. It is not by accident, however, that clowns fall without hurting themselves, hit themselves and others without bodily harm, land safely in nets, hang from apparatus, slide, teeter and tumble, all without injury. They may look awkward, and pantomime pain as part of their act, but they are skilled performers. This means that a clown must be trained and prepared.

A gymnastic clown, for example, should be a gymnast and a good one. Other clowns may not require intensive training as a gymnast does, but they should take their roles seriously, studying them carefully, perfecting actions and timing so that the success of the skit is guaranteed.

## Suggestions for the Clown

The amateur clown will be self-conscious at first, and it sometimes helps if the performer can forget that he* is Joseph Brown and remember that he is Joe the Clown. The clown is a medium, and the audience is not so interested in who the clown is, as in what he does and how he does it.

Overacting is a fault of many clowns. To be true, the gestures and actions must be generous and slowly done, but generally speaking, clown acts build up to a punch line, or blackout, or chase-off; and the unobtrusive teamwork of all, the coordinated routine, is more important than the "starry" performance of individuals. Let the stunt or punch line put the laugh across.

Clowns should not try to be silly, for clowning is a dignified art and profession. Clowns should omit anything off-color or offensive. Costumes, words or actions that are in bad taste, or that ridicule any race or nationality, have no place in a good clown act.

---

*Throughout this book, the words *he, him* and *his* are intended to mean also *she, her* and *hers,* to include all people, regardless of sex.

The amateur clown finds it difficult to realize that all action is *planned* action. The professional clown does not leave laughs to chance. It is sound advice to be seen only when there is something specific to do. Hence all clown acts should be written out in full detail and should be rehearsed until actions (and words) are exact. As much practice and rehearsal should go into each separate clown skit as goes into any other program number.

The clown should be alert to discover, make and create gadgets which become part of his own personal properties and part and parcel of his clown persona. Included in equipment of this nature one finds, for example, a nose that lights up, a lapel flower that squirts water, a shirt-front that curls, a cane with a bulb-horn on the handle, a mismatched pair of spats, and so on.

## Pantomime:

Whereas the spoken word is the chief medium of communication between an actor and his audience, the clown must rely mainly on pantomime, which is acting without words.

The clown depends, therefore, on gestures to interpret what he is doing and thinking, and such gestures are exaggerations or caricatures of normal action and movement.

If the clown is happy, he not only smiles broadly, he jumps up and down, hugs himself, and may turn cartwheels.

If he is sad, he sits down with his head between his knees, shakes all over from sobbing and finally takes out a big red bandanna handkerchief and starts to blow his nose, but there is a big hole in the handkerchief. Other traditional clown pantomimes are these:

**Running:** Work arms like pistons, bring knees up to chest, pause to indicate breathlessness. Don't cover too much space; run in place.

**Pain:** If struck by an object, fall or jump in direction propelled by instrument. If hit in the seat, arch body with head and legs extended backward. If struck on the head, stagger forward like a chicken trying to catch up to its head. Open mouth widely and yell, or act as if yelling, while placing hands on sore spot.

**Odors:** Hold nose.

**Pleasure:** Clap hands, click heels together, at same time jumping in air. Food — rub stomach.

**Fear:** Cower, cover head with arm or hide behind a person or object. Shake and tremble.

**Anticipation:** Gnaw fingernails. Clench and open hands, lean forward.

**Rage:** Jump up and down. Strike self on chest with fists or hit head against object.

**Pride:** Puff out chest, put thumbs in imaginary suspenders and spread hands, palms out.

Remember that all movements are bigger than life and that make-up masks facial expression. Hence the body must be the interpreter.

## Clown Types:

In the world of professional clowns, there are three classic types of clown characters developed over the centuries. All present-day clowns are modern variations of these types:

**The Whiteface Clown:** He is the classic Pierrot, a harlequin clown. His face is all white with the features painted on in black and red. When the features of this clown face are all of relatively normal size, the clown is called a *Neat Whiteface*. If the features are extra large, this clown is called a *Grotesque Whiteface*.

**The Auguste Clown:** This is the typical clown pictured in storybooks and circus posters. This clown face has a base color that is pink or reddish rather than pure white. Features are in red and black and are usually exaggerated in size. The mouth is thickly accented with white, which is also used around the eyes. Clothes are too large or small with wildly mismatched patterns.

**The Character Clown:** There is a lot of variation within this type. He may be a sad-faced hobo or tramp or maybe a happy, offbeat character with a big nose, funny mustache, crazy haircut or funny costume à la Charley Chaplin or some TV comics. The most popular character clown types used by nonprofessionals are: *Rube, Hobo (or Tramp), Policeman.*

## Costumes:

It is a wise investment for an organization that conducts one or more shows annually to own its suits. These should be repaired, dry-cleaned and stored after every show. Traditional suits include the following types:

**Whiteface:** This is a court jester or Pierrot type of suit. It may be purchased, rented or made. Dressmaker patterns are available. See local stores selling patterns. Cambric or cotton is suitable material. It should be colorful. Make it full, ample, baggy.

**Auguste:** Suspenders, oversize shoes, tie, etc. Clothes are too large or small with wildly mismatched patterns and colors. Pants are too short, socks show. Wild wig with tiny or huge hat optional.

**Rube:** Overalls, braces, plaid shirt, old broad-brimmed straw hat, red bandanna handkerchief for scarf.

**Hobo:** Large, sloppy, worn shoes, with holes in soles. Baggy, dark trousers with colored patches on seat and knees. Sloppy coat with many pockets, a bright red or yellow vest. Derby or silk hat with no top to it. Wig optional.

**Policeman:** Blue uniform and brass buttons à la Gilbert and Sullivan. Policeman's hat should be that of an English bobby (19th century). Policeman's billy club and metal badge of office.

## Make-Up:

Clowns should study pictures and photographs of professional clowns and proceed to develop their own facial make-up. Experience is the best teacher, and clowns should spend much time practicing the art of making up their faces. Strive for individuality.

Make-up materials may be obtained from any theatrical supply house:

- cream or cake make-up (various shades to suit character parts)
- colored pencils and liners (red, blue, black, yellow, white)

9

- minstrel black
- tooth wax
- spirit gum
- rubber and foam noses
- cold cream
- powder and powder puffs
- clown white

Put the costume on after the make-up is completed. Protect clothes with a cloth around the shoulders similar to a barber's spread. Place a towel on the lap, and sit before a mirror. Wear skull cap.

Spread clown white over all exposed parts of face, neck, ears. With a dull stick mark out the lines and areas to be colored. From these areas remove excess clown white with a bit of cloth.

Use pencils and liners for coloring job. Powder over first layer, then put on a second coloring coat.

Keep lines and colored markings to a minimum. Accentuate not more than two features, such as the nose and mouth.

After make-up is on, add a wig, hat, false ears, nose and so on. Nose putty, if used, should go on first. Spirit gum will hold beard and mustache. First, remove all grease and dirt. Hold in place until set.

Use cold cream for removing make-up. Rub it in well, then erase with paper towel. Follow up with warm water and soap.

To make up a hobo or other character, use a cold-cream base. For the tramp, the base color should be dark sunburn. Use black make-up for heavy eyebrows. Beard and mustache effect may be obtained from dark gray make-up.

Do not color tramp's lips; rather, accentuate bags under eyes or hollow cheeks, using dark browns or reds.

If possible, obtain the assistance of people who have had theatrical make-up experience and put them in charge of supplies and making up clowns and other characters.

It is worthwhile having make-up boxes, one for each dressing room.

Mirrors, stools and make-up illustrations should be placed in make-up dressing room.

## CHAPTER 2

# Program & Organization

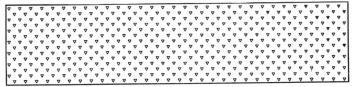

Clown acts may be scheduled for many types of occasions, such as special programs, exhibits, demonstrations and contests. Intermissions at such programs provide opportunities for planned clowning, and such breaks add color and interest to the program.

The Indoor Circus and Gym Show is an ideal example of such a program, because it provides an intermission or break between each act during which a series of clown acts may be presented. Such an elaborate program requires careful organization. The following sample program and suggestions for its organization may be modified or adapted for less elaborate productions.

## Sample Program of an Indoor Circus and Gym Show

1. Grand Entry
   A simple march by all participants
   Massed singing of national anthem with flag-raising
   Crowning of Circus Queen

2. Our Junior Members
   This may be:
   - drill team
   - pajama and candle parade
   - group games and relays
   - Indian dance or powwow

3. Clown Act

4. Tired Tumblers
   Junior or intermediate-age tumblers

5. Clown Act

6. The Highlander's or Sailor's Hornpipe
   Dance routine by one of the classes

7. Clown Act

8. Gymnastic Number
   - springboard and box horse
   - trampoline
   - clowns included

9. Specialty Number
   - dance team or
   - chariot race, or magician, etc.

10. Clown Act

11. Pyramids
    Senior performers on parallel bars, or table and chair, or ladder pyramids

12. Intermission (Concession Sales)

13. Gymnastics
    - high bars
    - flying rings
    - trapeze, etc.
    - clowns included

14. Clown Act

15. Demonstration
    - judo, or
    - weightlifting, or
    - wrestling or fencing

16. Clown Act

17. Tap Dance Routines

18. Clown Act

19. The Animals Come to Town
    - use animals for the occasion
    - clowns are included

20. Gymnastics or Pyramids, or Hand-Balancing

21. Clown Act

22. Class Drill
    - calisthenics
    - Indian clubs
    - boom drill
    - precision marching

23. Clown Act

24. Statuary

25. Grand Finale
    - ensemble of complete cast

# Planning Committee

Any sizable event will require a planning committee and a director. The committee should have a chairperson, and its members should consist of the chairpersons of three major subcommittees — program, publicity and finance.

The director of the show may be the recreation director of the organization, or the director of physical education. He is also a logical person to be chairman of the program committee.

The planning committee decides first of all upon the objectives of the show. Is it to be a demonstration of the program? a money-raiser? the climax of a season? a holiday celebration? The answers to such questions will determine the type of program to be planned.

The committee should be formed several months in advance in order that dates, location, theme and so on may be determined early, a proper timetable developed, and all concerned properly informed. In general, the committee is adult-structured, whereas the program is aimed to appeal to all age levels.

At first, meetings should be held monthly, then weekly as the circus becomes imminent.

A description of the functions of the three major subcommittees follows.

The secret of program success is to involve people — individuals and groups. The director and committee should seek out members with particular and peculiar talents who can provide specialty numbers, such as juggling, unicycling, tight-wire performers, magicians. Nor should clubs and classes be overlooked, since their members should be encouraged to develop skits and stunts.

Adequate preparation and training must go into all phases of a program to ensure that a show is entertaining and high-quality.

Usually the director carries the initial responsibility for presenting a skeleton program to the planning committee. Once this basic outline is approved, the program committee as a whole accepts or rejects future ideas. The program committee will be concerned with a theme and the order of events.

Subcommittees of the program committee are: House, Costumes, Music, Clowns, Scene-Shifters.

**House Committee:** Where will the show be held?
General plan: Floor space and seating.
Seating: Extra chairs or bleachers. Seats to be obtained, delivered at set date, and returned day after show.
Ushers: Number required. Uniforms. Training and instructions.
Fire prevention: Check all extinguishers and fire hose. Check exits. Invite fire marshal to inspect.
Male and female attendants or chaperones for dressing rooms.
Valuables: Arrange for performers to check valuables.
Properties: This function is unnecessary if the committee on clowns (see

***Clowns Committee*)** looks after clown properties and if someone in each act is named to assume this responsibility for his or her program. A list of all properties should be made for each and every act. Properties should be placed in a selected spot and checked before all performances. Damaged props should be repaired. Borrowed props should be returned in good condition.

***Costumes Committee:*** Determine types and numbers of costumes required.
Check against stock.
Check for cleanliness and repairs.
Arrange to rent, buy or make costumes not on hand.
Arrange for fittings.
For show periods, have dressing room assistants on hand with thread, needles and irons, for emergency repairs.
After show: Collect, clean and store owned costumes. Return rented costumes.
Note: Clean, attractive, well-designed costumes with pleasing color harmonies are a *must*. A well-dressed act is halfway to success.
If program numbers require make-up, this may be an added responsibility of the costume committee. Supplies may be obtained from theatrical and costume houses.

***Music Committee:*** Plan and arrange for some type of music for the acts: piano, small band, accordion, clown band or music through records and public-address systems.
Regardless of the means by which music is provided, it is invaluable for the atmosphere it creates for background and fill-ins, before the show and between acts, and for accompanying drills, marches and dances.
One person should be appointed director of music. A cue sheet should be supplied so the director can coordinate music with the program.

***Clowns Committee:*** Responsible for the following details:
- selecting and training clowns
- choosing material (skits, stunts, *etc.*)
- taking care of costumes (clear with costume committee)
- obtaining props for acts
- obtaining make-up materials
- obtaining make-up person to be on duty each night
- doing emergency repairs (see ***Costumes Committee***)
- obtaining special clown and props room
A clown captain is recommended. This may be a nonclown, someone from the committee, for instance, whose duties are to time the acts, call clowns on and off, watch that clowns do not steal or detract from other acts, and do similar tasks.

***Scene-Shifters Committee:*** Five or six roustabouts or hustlers under a captain are invaluable. They set up and remove apparatus and scenes.

A floor plan should be provided, and equipment listed for each event.

Costume them in sneakers, brown or blue denims, and matching T-shirts
or sport shirts.

Scene-shifters should be out of sight except when performing duties.

A leaders club sometimes accepts this responsibility.

## Publicity Committee:

A special event such as an indoor circus requires an audience. Promoting and publicizing the event through all possible media is highly important. Members of this committee must be carefully selected, because they will have a long, hard job. Publicity and promotion of the event should start early, and become more and more intensive as the date grows nearer.

The following outline of the scope and duties of this committee may indicate a need for subcommittees:

- Tradition and word of mouth are top media for spreading information.

- Newspaper, radio and TV

- Brief news release after each meeting of the planning committee

- Special weekender features when circus is one month away, up to the date of the program

- Live broadcasts of practice sessions

- Feature articles on "stars" and human interest stories

- Photographs

- Posters and handbills: Handbills may be delivered to homes and/or schools, or laid on tables of service club luncheons. Avoid pictures of live animals if they are not to be present in the actual show. A poster contest may be conducted for the youngsters.

- Other media: Pictures in lobby or store windows, banners on building front or across street, store-window cards, streetcar or bus advertising, displays by art classes and vocational classes, a parade, announcements on motion picture screens, decorating building in keeping with circus theme (Arabian Nights, Wild West, South Seas, etc.).

- Printed or mimeographed programs: The program lists, in order, the events, along with names of performers or groups or classes. These are distributed by the ushers.

## Finance Committee:

A member of the finance committee may be selected as treasurer, but regardless of method, a treasurer is a must and so is a budget. There should be an overall budget approved by the planning committee. and each subcommittee must operate within its allocation.

Once price of admission is determined and tickets are printed (two months in advance), a sales plan should be developed and put into action four weeks ahead of the show.

Contests to discover the best ticket-seller or the best teams of salespeople are popular, and appropriate prizes are offered.

If the program folder is also a money-raiser by means of solicited paid advertising, this, too, is an item for the finance committee. Prices should be obtained from several printing firms on tickets and programs.

If there are to be concessions, a subcommittee of the finance committee may be appointed.

Concessions consist of games of chance and/or skill. The committee plans the booths and layout, checks on the games, prizes and other details, and arranges for operators and bankers. It is advisable that tickets be sold at a central location, thus avoiding the handling of money in connection with the games.

Other concessions may include candy, ice cream, drinks, popcorn and hot dogs. If hawkers circulate among the audience, they should wear uniforms. These salespeople must be advised when and where not to sell.

A financial statement should be turned over to the planning committee after the show, and this should be saved for the next year's committee.

## The Master of Ceremonies

The master of ceremonies (M.C.) is much more than a figurehead, for he and the director are key people in the timing, promotion and general success of the show. Hence care should be exercised in selecting an M.C.

Experience is desirable. Other such qualities include personal appearance, appreciation of showmanship, good voice, sense of humor, friendly leadership.

The master of ceremonies in a circus setting is the ringmaster. Here the recommended costume is a full riding habit, dress hat and diagonal red band across the chest.

The ringmaster welcomes the guests and introduces the acts with flamboyant gestures and extravagant expressions. A whip that cracks may give emphasis to his remarks. A flowing mustache is part of a male ringmaster's make-up.

The ringmaster may well become an actor, especially as a trainer in animal acts. His position is a respected one, and he should not be treated as a clown.

It is helpful for the M.C. to familiarize himself with the acts and the actors.

Unless he participates in an act, the M.C. is offstage when acts are on.

# Training Clowns

There are several books at your library that will provide some basic training for beginners, but one of the best ways to get started if you have a large group is to look at some filmstrips together. They provide an excellent base for group discussion. The best filmstrips on clowning are available from: Contemporary Drama Service, 885 Elkton Drive, Colorado Springs, Colorado 80907. Especially recommended are *Be a Clown* and *Clowning for Kids.* For those interested in religious clowning, Contemporary Drama also offers *An Introduction to Clown Ministry* and *The Art of Pantomime in Church.* If you need videotapes instead of filmstrips, inquire from Contemporary Drama Service to see if they are currently available.

# Production Suggestions

Present a peppy show. A well-paced show of 1½ hours with continuous action is better than one that is slower and longer.

The second half of the show should be paced slightly faster than the first half. It is also helpful to use the intermission period to set up any elaborate equipment and to schedule such acts early in this second session.

The most spectacular event should be saved for last so that the audience goes away with the best impression.

Cue sheets should be provided for the announcer, director, doormen, scene-shifters (post near equipment depot) and person in charge of lighting.

A rehearsal night is advised. To provide a live audience, invite children from orphanages or children's homes to be nonpaying guests. A service club might sponsor such youngsters and supply refreshments, too.

The crowning of a circus queen is worthwhile.

Intermission may be an appropriate time to present annual awards and recognitions to champion athletes or volunteers.

A precircus parade draws attention in smaller communities.

Something must be happening every minute.

# After the Show Is Over

***Clean-up Squad:*** Return equipment and restore everything to original condition.

Scrub floors.

***Evaluation Meeting:*** Planning committee meets for final report, and recommendations are made and filed for next year.

Decisions are made for disposal of surplus funds.

***Bread-and-Butter Notes:*** Thank-you letters are sent by the director to all who assisted, loaned equipment or helped in any way.

An honorary circus membership card may be mailed to all participants.

***Circus Banquet:*** Honor performers and champion ticket-sellers.

Provide entertainment (circus movie).

Tell participants how profits will be used.

CHAPTER 3

# Clown Equipment

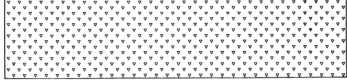

Reference to clown equipment has been made in the chapter on Program & Organization, in the outline of the duties of the costumes committee and the clowns committee.

## Properties

In addition to costumes, a props room and a props supervisor, clowns require certain mechanical aids or gadgets. There are many standard pieces of equipment of this type that should be found in the clowns' props room. Much of this can be produced by handymen or by crafts or hobby departments, and other items may be purchased or rented. The classified "Yellow Pages" of any large city telephone directory are helpful in ordering many of the following items:

**Siren or Gong:** Sirens may be obtained from automobile supply houses, fire departments, or novelty or magic supply houses. (See the "Yellow Pages" for the latter — under Novelties or Party Favors.) An old car brake drum makes a satisfactory gong if struck with a metal hammer. Records that produce all kinds of noises are available, and these can be played over a public-address system.

**Fake Noses, Ears:** See Costume Rentals and Theatrical Equipment and Supplies in the classified section of the telephone directory.

**Beards, Wigs, Mustaches, False Faces:** See Costume Rentals and Theatrical Equipment and Supplies, and Party Favors and Novelties, in the classified section of the telephone directory.

**Noise-Makers:** See the same source as above.

**Papier Mâché Heads:** See the same source as above.

**Swat Sticks:** These are used for comedy "paddling." Being made of light wood, they produce a sound that is much worse than the hit. Young clowns should be instructed that the seat is the only permissible striking area. Indiscriminate use could cause injury. Two sticks — 30 inches long, 3 inches wide and ¼-inch thick — are screwed together at one end to form a handle. Approximately at the midpoint, a ¼-inch wedge is fastened to one slat so as to spread the open ends. The ends clap together whenever an object is struck.

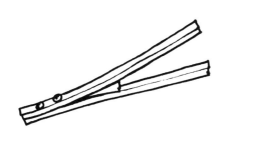

**Firecracker:** Empty a 48-ounce fruit juice can by puncturing a hole in the top center and a small air hole at the side. When the can is drained and dry, and after removing its label, paint the can red. Stick a "dynamite fuse" of heavy cord in the center hole, having plugged the other hole if necessary.

***Bomb:*** This can be a large bowling ball with the thumb and finger holes filled in after a make-believe fuse has been inserted in one of these. A fresh coat of black paint may make the bomb appear more realistic. A laceless volleyball painted black may be substituted. Use an old ball.

***Telephone:*** Don't be modern. An old-fashioned dummy phone will do. This can be made up from spools and scraps of wood. Paint flat black.

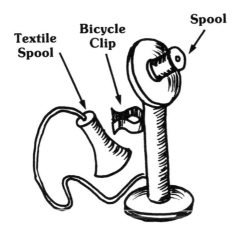

**Spool**

**Bicycle
Clip**

**Textile
Spool**

***Shoes:*** Clown shoes should be about 22 inches long and 5 inches wide. Screw or cleat an old pair of shoes to a piece of plywood, above size. Build up false toes with canvas, then paint the shoes.

***Skull Caps:*** Most clowns wear a skull cap that is neutral in color. These can be made from the tops of silk or nylon stockings. Eight or 10 inches are cut off the top of the stocking; a knot is tied at the ragged end. This makes a cap after slits are cut for ears.

***Guns:*** Wooden guns may be made by tracing a cardboard pattern from a real gun and cutting a traced gun from one-inch plywood. Guns should be painted.

**Policeman's Billy:** Use black cloth or canvas sewed in a tube shape about 15 inches long. This is stuffed with kapok or light insulating material. A leather thong or lace may be fastened through one end.

**Clown House:** A clown house is made from 2 x 2's with hinges at all corners, so that it may be folded and stored. A good size is 7 x 7 x 7 feet. Cover frames with wallboard, then paint or paper. Two doors and two windows opposite one another permit diving in and out. No roof is needed.

## Circus Animals

From a fundamental *H* form of construction, but with two cross-bars, a number of animals may be built. This structure provides space for two operators and the four legs; and the long sides of the *H* rest on their shoulders. Naturally, the legs of the performers should be costumed in burlap or tight-fitting denim trousers and painted to harmonize with the characteristics of the animal portrayed.

Overall length is about 6 feet; width from *A* to *B*, about 22 inches.

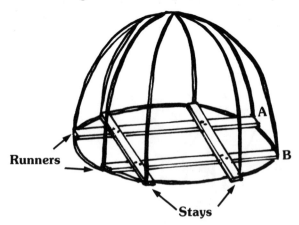

Use light wood (pine) for basic structure. Stiff wire may be used for the framework, or use light lathes which have been soaked in water to make them pliable. Barrel hoops may also be used to form the body.

Cover framework with burlap or canvas. Use water-soluble paint for coloring.

More care should be given the animal's head which, in the case of a long-necked creature such as the giraffe, is carried on a long pole by the first operator. A hole must be provided in the body for the pole.

Cords leading to the head enable the operator to move the animal's head or mouth. A flashlight battery connection to illuminate the eyes is another consideration.

Provide seeing and breathing space for performers.

Animals most readily constructed include the elephant, horse, giraffe and world's greatest freak.

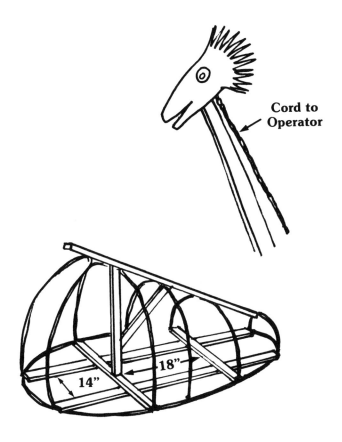

**Cord to Operator**

18"

14"

## Using the Animals

If there are enough animals, an animal training act may be presented under the direction of an animal trainer or ringmaster.

A one-, two- or three-ring show may be preceded by a march in to circus band music (records are available). The trainer cracks his whip and gets the animals to mount their boxes and barrels for a pose.

*From *How to Put On an Amateur Circus,* Fred Hacker and Prescott Eames (Minneapolis: T.S. Denison and Company, 1955).

In addition to constructed animals of the four-footed type, there may be others such as monkeys, seals and bears, for which costumes may be rented.

There is always one animal that never quite does what he is supposed to do, or does it when he is not supposed to do it. This creature begs for tidbits thrown to him by the trainer.

When an animal sits down, the front man sits in the rear man's lap.

Animals lie down, roll over, pick out the prettiest girl in the audience.

They answer questions *yes* or *no* by shaking or nodding the head.

Arithmetic questions are answered by stamping with the feet. The animal doesn't stop counting when he is asked to tell someone's age. In fact, he stamps with all four feet.

The elephant can perch on a barrel, or walk around it with two feet on the barrel and two feet off.

A novelty act for a cow includes much of the above such as counting or answering questions, but this cow gives white milk when milked from one side and chocolate milk from the other.

Seals balance balls or balloons on their noses. They accidentally sit on balloons, causing them to explode. Seals can have fun on a slide. (Floor in front should be well-waxed.)

Bears in pairs can do a simple polka to music. Bears may roller-skate on hind legs. It is more difficult if done on four legs.

Monkeys may do mat or trampoline tricks.

Hoops covered with paper are useful for jumping through.

A Hula Hoop number by the animals might be considered.

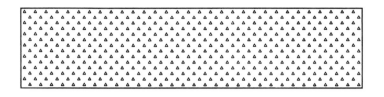

CHAPTER 4

# Walk-Ons & Walk-Arounds

# What Are Walk-Ons
# and Walk-Arounds?

Answer: They are just about what the chapter title implies.

If there is one performer, he generally walks onto the stage or floor area and completes, often without stopping, a circling tour, exiting at the original entrance. This is a walk-around. If he does not need to make the complete circle for his act, it is a walk-on. Both are "quickies."

If there is more than one performer, the extras are usually trailers.

Walk-ons and walk-arounds rely mainly on pantomime. They are adaptable to individual skills.

They may be built up through repetition, providing slight variations are planned for the repeats.

Walk-ons are not considered complete clown acts and may or may not be written into the program.

# When?

These stunts are best used when the timing of the general show so indicates, and the M.C. or clown director should be responsible for running in an act when needed.

A walk-on makes a good fill-in when there is a lull or delay in the program.

Besides being used as fill-ins, walk-ons provide diversions between acts and are particularly useful during scene changes. It is always more entertaining to watch clowns than stagehands.

Usually one walk-on at a time will suffice. However, there are alternate possibilities. For example, two or three walk-ons may follow in rapid succession, and two or three minutes may be filled in this way, but this should be the maximum amount of time allowed.

A second alternative is to have a simultaneous entry of two or three walk-ons, with each performer going his own merry way as though no act were in progress.

Still another acceptable time for these stunts is during an apparatus display, particularly if the caliber of performance is such that it is not of center-ring standard.

This or any other clown act should never be "floored" when it might distract from a worthwhile performance or distract the performers so that they do less than their best.

## Acts for Walk-Ons and Walk-Arounds

# #1 Announcements

"Announcements" such as the following may be used for fill-in whenever there is a slight delay in the program.

Clown rushes in and waves his arms for silence, then makes announcement in all seriousness. Or the clown's entrance may be preceded by a fanfare, or a clown quartet may sing over the P.A.: "A-nounce-ments, a-nounce – ments, a-nounce — ments!" Or, "It's an awful death to die, it's an awful death to die, it's an awful death to be talked to death, it's an awful death to die."

**ANNOUNCEMENT 1:**
Ladies and gentlemen, I have been asked to announce that after Monday, Tuesday and Wednesday there will follow Thursday, Friday and Saturday. I thank you.

**ANNOUNCEMENT 2:**
Ladies and gentlemen, I have been asked to announce that the owner of car license number _____ has left his lights burning *(clown rushes in and whispers in announcer's ear)*, and the left rear tire is flat *(another clown repeats whispering business)*, and the motor is running *(another clown appears),* and furthermore, you are in a no-parking area *(another clown)*, but you don't have to worry about your car being stolen because the police are there *(final clown)*, and your wife just phoned to say you didn't do the dishes before leaving.

**ANNOUNCEMENT 3:**
Ladies and gentlemen, I have been asked by the management to make this most important announcement: "Will the audience please keep its seats while the crowd passes out."

**ANNOUNCEMENT 4:**
Ladies and gentlemen, there is an angry and armed man out in the hall
who says his wife is in here with another man and if that man doesn't
come out now he's coming in to shoot. *(Clowns who have seated themselves in the audience run out frantically.)*

# #2 Dog & Horn

First clown circles the floor with a real dog on leash.
First clown goes round again, a second clown trailing. The second clown
has a horn or trumpet. He also has a horn or trumpet reed hidden in
his mouth.
Whenever the first clown stops, the second clown holds the horn to the
mouth of the dog, who apparently blows the horn.
Clowns are very much pleased and are proud of their dog. They repeat
the stunt a number of times.

# #3 Egg & Feather

A clown with a built-up putty-nose circles the floor.
The clown attempts some simple balancing or juggling feats.
The clown produces a handsome feather which he balances on the end
of his nose by sticking the quill into the putty.
An egg is similarly balanced. *(The egg has been blown and has a needle
projecting through it far enough to hold in the putty.)*

# #4 Fire Department, Please!

During an exhibition of apparatus work a clown rushes across the floor
carrying a cupful of water. He likewise rushes to the exit. This happens
several times in a very few minutes.
Sometimes the clown makes the trip with only a few drops spilled; other
times he trips on the mats and has to go back for more water.

**Ringmaster:**
*(Finally intervenes. Stops the clown.)* What's the matter?

**Clown:**
Don't stop me now, mister; my dressing room is on fire!

# #5 Fresh Fish

A clown stands beside a piano on top of which there is a large bowl of goldfish.
During an act for which a pianist is required, the clown will occasionally
dip his hand into the bowl as though trying to catch a fish. On catching
a goldfish, he holds it by the tail. After the fish squirms a couple of
times, the clown pops it into his mouth.
The clown does this nonchalantly, giving his undivided attention to the
pianist. The stunt is repeated several times. *(Besides live goldfish, the
bowl contains fine strips of raw carrot which have been cut in the
shape of goldfish. The clown eats the imitations.)*

# #6 Fly & Bladder

A large artificial fly is attached to the end of a wire, and the other end of
the wire goes down the clown's back, being looped over the clown's
head so that the fly appears to be suspended or flying ahead.
The clown carries a light cane on the end of which there is an inflated bladder
or balloon. He walks around swatting at the fly with the balloon. He
misses quite frequently, striking other clowns or youngsters in the
audience.

# #7 The Golfer

A clown dressed as an eccentric golfer has a bag full of odd clubs.
He demonstrates "trick" shots as he moves about:
   A. Tee-up ball. Swing and miss. Change tee for a higher one. Repeat.
      Change tees until they are knee-high.
   B. Use a club with huge head *(the never-miss)* to drive plastic ball into
      the crowd.
   C. Use a telescopic club for playing out-of-bounds ball.
   D. Use a club with a rubber shaft. It wraps itself around the golfer.
   E. Use a club with a loose head which flies off. The head is controlled
      by a length of cord.

# #8 Hair! Hair!

Clown walks around, balancing various objects — wand, chair, a medicine
ball fastened to the top of a vaulting pole, etc.
He interrupts this routine to steal a hair from the ringmaster's or a clown's

head. He proceeds to balance this imaginary hair on his forehead. Consequently, he does considerable head-scratching.

# #9 Henpecked Henry

**PROPS:**
An umbrella
A small but loud whistle
A number of specially prepared parcels

**ACTION:**
Fat lady clown enters, followed by Henpecked Henry. She carries an umbrella. He is loaded down with numerous parcels.

Every few steps Henry drops one or more parcels. Each time he lets out a whistle from the one hidden in his lips. Each time she stops and returns, and as Henry picks up the parcel, she hits him over the head with the umbrella.

This is repeated around the hall.

Finally, when they are near a selected part of the audience, Henry asserts himself.

He gives a terrific blast on the whistle and drops all the parcels. These he picks up, one at a time, and throws them at his wife.

She is between Henry and the audience, and like a skilled boxer she ducks all the missiles, which fly into the crowd.

Parcels are very light, having been filled with kapoc, cotton batten or inflated balloons.

There can be a few "plants" in the audience who receive certain bundles, which they open for the amusement of those present.

# #10 Juggling I

**PROPS:**
Three brightly colored balls — two hard, one rubber

**ACTION:**
Clown juggler circles the floor. En route, he juggles the three balls.

Clown juggler breaks the routine by throwing the rubber ball high in the air. It bounces on the clown's head as he simultaneously clicks the two hard *(metallic)* balls together.

Continue act.

The clown is deadpan throughout.

As an unsolicited encore he returns wearing a hat with a trick top. A fourth ball is concealed in the clown's mouth.

The three-ball juggling act is repeated, but this time the ball that is thrown high is caught in the hat as the clown spits out the fourth ball.

The clown may continue juggling, or he may take a bow, causing the ball to roll out of the hat.

# #11 Juggling II

**PROPS:**
A metal tray on the bottom of which a ring is soldered (hole in the ring, about one inch in diameter)
Rods or poles of various lengths
A number of glasses and one or two soft-drink bottles
An identical fake tray with glasses and bottles fastened to it so that they cannot fall off — the whole attached to the end of a very long rod

**ACTION:**
Clown juggler enters balancing tray and glasses on top of rod. *(Rod fits in ring.)*
Clown serves one or two customers a drink.
Repeat between future acts, but each time with longer rod. *(Juggler may require assistance in getting tray off rod.)*
Finally clown enters with fake tray and glasses. Much teetering and tottering, with the whole thing being spilled over the audience *(nothing in bottles this time)*.

# #12 Look at It Now!

A clown equipped with a toy balloon makes himself comfortable in a conspicuous spot. Here he proceeds to inflate the balloon.
From time to time he holds the balloon at arm's length and exclaims enthusiastically and admiringly, *"Look at it now!"*
Inflection and emphasis should build up with the increasing size of the balloon.
Finally the balloon bursts; and the clown, tearfully and disconsolately, emits his last *"Look at it now!"*

# #13 Other Ideas

A. Clown or clowns walk around on stilts.
B. A clown overburdened with packages follows a female clown about the floor. Parcels slip and fall, and the clown has to pick them up. As fast as he recovers a parcel, another one falls to the floor. In exasperation the female clown chases the package-carrying clown off.

35

C. A foolish clown trips on a mat and finds he has lost a thumb which he flexes against the palm of his hand. He counts fingers, up to four, and recounts. He looks under mat, etc. Other clowns may join in helping the foolish one. A second clown strikes the foolish one over the head with a slapstick, and the thumb pops up.

# #14 Paradise Lost — Paradise Found

First clown circles the floor reading a huge book. *(This book may be made from heavy cardboard or thin plywood. A book of sample wall-papers is ideal.)*
Title on front cover in large letters: PARADISE LOST.
This clown may wear large horn-rimmed glasses and a mortarboard.
Second clown follows in a few seconds.
He carries a huge pair of dice. Sign on second clown's back: PARADISE FOUND.

# #15 The Peppydent Smile

*(A clown prepares himself by blacking out his teeth with black theatrical wax. He next inserts a set of false buck teeth obtainable from a trick store. Hidden in his mouth are a number of white beans.)*
The clown smiles broadly on entering, making sure all see his "store" teeth.
The clown becomes interested in a tumbling act and decides to do a stunt. He runs, trips on the mat, and falls flat on his face.
He sits up, holding his hand to his mouth, and secretly removes the false teeth.
He discovers loose teeth and spits them *(the beans)* out one at a time.
He takes out a mirror and is at first horrified by his appearance *(no teeth)*, but then is pleased. He exits grinning broadly.

# #16 A Perfect Pedestrian

A hobo clown wanders about, wearing the following accessories:
- old-fashioned bulb auto horn on hat
- green light on right sleeve
- red light on left sleeve
- an auto headlight on each hand, illuminated from battery under coat

- rear bumper
- sign in front: A PERFECT PEDESTRIAN
- sign in back: IN CASE OF ACCIDENT, PHONE LOOKOUT 1 2 3-OUCH!
- first aid kit may be added

# #17 Self-Service

A hobo clown saunters around the floor.

From a small suitcase or briefcase, he takes out a blowtorch. From his vest pocket he selects an expensive cigar wrapper. Opening it, he removes a wiener or hot dog.

Unscrewing the end of his cane he places the hot dog on a spike set under the cap. Clown lights the blowtorch from a cigarette lighter and proceeds to cook himself a meal.

He takes a roll from the false top of his silk hat. Salt and pepper shakers come from pockets, and from a plastic container, the clown squirts mustard or ketchup on the hot dog.

His pocket handkerchief turns out to be a paper napkin. Clown walks off eating his lunch.

# #18 Snake Charmer

During a gymnastic or tumbling number, a clown, wearing a towel turban on his head and an Indian blanket draped over his shoulders, sits down in front of a round wicker basket open at the top.

In Indian sitting position, the clown takes out a flute and begins to play. *(If clown cannot play the flute, recorded music can be piped in.)*

A snake gradually rises from the basket and sways to and fro with the music. *(The snake is imitation and is controlled by a fine black thread running from the snake's head through a hole in the end of the flute and into the clown's right hand. The clown holds the flute in his left hand.)*

# #19 A Stretcher Case

**PROPS:**

A stretcher is made from two long rods or poles which are held in their relative places by a number of barrel hoops fastened to them.

A sheet or blanket and a pair of gym shoes

The sheet thrown over the barrel hoops gives the appearance of a body on the stretcher.

Running shoes are fastened to the frame so as to protrude at one end. These are the victim's feet.

**ACTION:**

This is a walk-around.

Two men carry the stretcher, and the head of the rear carrier is also the victim's head.

The rear man throws his head well back and grasps the stretcher in a manner most likely to add to the illusion *(rods on shoulders)*.

Front man also has stretcher rods over his shoulders. He is deadpan. He never stops or looks to the left or right.

The rear man, or victim, however, rolls his head and eyes to look at the pretty girls.

A very pretty girl stops him in his tracks. He stands still, then runs to get back into position.

# #20 Why Men Leave Home

**PROPS:**

Round metal washtub with rope shoulder straps

Sign: WHY MEN LEAVE HOME

Sign: WASH-DAY BLUES

Doll that cries *mama*

Washboard, soap, water, number of diapers

**ACTION:**

This is a walk-around.

Small clown leads, carrying a sign: WASH-DAY BLUES.

Second clown follows, wearing the washtub. He is busy with soap, diapers and washboard.

Sign on second clown's back: WHY MEN LEAVE HOME.

Third clown follows with mama doll.

The doll cries. Clown looks apprehensive. After testing, he removes a diaper and throws it into the washtub.

The doll wears about a dozen diapers so that the action is almost continuous throughout the walk-around.

If desired, a small clothesline can be attached to wooden uprights on the sides of the washtub. The washerman hangs up the laundry as he goes, extracting clothespins from his bosom.

At length the third clown has had too many wet diapers and he throws baby and all into the tub.

CHAPTER 5

# Clown Acts with Simple Equipment

# #21 Baseball

(See also "Play Ball," No. 91.)

**PROPS:**

Slapstick for bat                         One softball
One telescope

**ACTION:**

Clowns run on baseball field and warm up for game. They use make-believe
ball. Catcher slaps hands on receiving catch and throws back to pitcher,
etc. Pitcher does slow reach-out on catching return.

First batter stands ready with slapstick.

"Play ball."

First pitch. Catcher signals. Pitcher nods head. Full wind-up and pitch.
Batter swings, misses, hits self, and falls down.

Second pitch. Slow motion. This is a hop ball. Catcher and batter indicate
by their eyes and motions of catcher's hands the action of the ball.
Strike two.

Third pitch. Catcher changes signals and, in order to stop pitcher, rushes
out of box to be hit in the pants by bat. The pitcher catches the
catcher. Catcher limps back.

Fourth pitch. Batter connects for a high, high hit. He tears round the
bases and as he passes each base-player, his speed knocks the
players' hats off, and they spin in place.

The batter slides safely home as fielders continue to gaze skyward.

The umpire takes telescope out of pocket. Follows flight of ball and passes
it round to players.

Pitcher, in following flight of ball, leans over backward until he falls flat on
his back and in a designated spot.

The designated spot is directly under a small box fastened to the roof.
The box has a bottom trap door with a string leading to the running
track or gallery.

An accomplice opens the trap. The pitcher catches the ball, and all exit
gleefully.

# #22 Be Nonchalant

**PROPS:**

Card table                       Chair

Newspaper

**CHARACTERS:**

Two clowns with tumbling ability

**ACTION:**

During a tumbling exhibition a clown makes himself comfortable with a front-row seat.

He places card table near mats and sits on a chair facing table and mats.

After a while he loses interest in the tumbling and starts to read a paper, becoming terribly engrossed in the contents.

A second clown becomes curious. The second clown walks around the first clown, reads over his shoulder, pulls his hair, and so on, without being noticed by him.

First clown has one elbow resting on the table. Second clown yanks away table, expecting first clown to fall off his chair.

First clown maintains his sitting posture, with elbow resting on air.

Second clown now jerks away the chair, but first clown's position remains unchanged.

Second clown takes a run from the rear of the first clown and dives over him, landing on the mat and taking the newspaper with him.

First clown is still frozen in sitting position, and hands are in same position as when reading the paper.

Second clown approaches first clown as though to push him over. Instead, he places his right foot in a cross-over motion on the first clown's thigh and does a half-turn-about, assuming an angel balance as first clown adjusts his position to be the under man.

Clowns do a short partner-balance routine.

# #23 Button Up

**PROPS:**

Some stage money                  Stopwatch (not essential)

**CHARACTERS:**

Three clowns                         Ringmaster

**ACTION:**

Two clowns enter; one wears a vest *(hobo clown)*.

First clown bets the other he can't unbutton his vest in 30 seconds.

The bet is taken, and each places a dollar on the floor.

The ringmaster times with stopwatch, and the vest is easily unbuttoned within the time limit. Winner picks up the money.

Winner goes to walk off but is called back.

The first clown this time bets five times the amount of the first bet that the second clown can't button *up* his vest in 30 seconds.

Bets are placed on the floor, and clown quickly buttons "down" his vest, starting with the top button.

Ringmaster again times.

The clown wearing the vest thinks he has won and stoops down to pick up the money.

The other clown kicks him, causing the "vested" clown to jump to his feet, leaving the money on the floor.

First clown doesn't let vested clown get away. He pantomimes, pointing to the buttons one at a time, that the vest was buttoned *down* and not *up.*

The final winner walks off, leaving the former winner scratching his head.

Another clown, wearing a vest, can enter, and the loser may seize upon him as a likely victim for the same hoax.

The first part of the stunt is repeated, but when the "goat" picks up the winnings and heads for the exit, he fails to return on signal from the real "goat."

# #24 Death, Where Is Thy Sting?

## PROPS:
Clown hammer (sponge rubber)
Small black casket on wheels with pull-string

## CHARACTERS:
Clown                                      Hobo clown
Two other clowns

## ACTION:
*(Two clowns enter. One of the two is a hobo who continually scratches himself.)*

**Second Clown:**
What's the matter with you?

**Hobo Clown:**
I'm going to sue that blankety-blank no-good railroad which just had the privilege of having me for a passenger.

**Second Clown:**
How come you're going to sue them?

**Hobo Clown:**
'Cause they've been carrying live stock in grain cars.

*(Second clown begins to help hobo take off his shirt, which is every color of the rainbow, and which may have various hotel towels fastened to tail. Two more clowns enter with casket and in time to help in the shirt business. When the shirt is off, clowns inspect seams for fleas. Each discovers one. One flea gets away and is rediscovered in audience.)*

**Hobo Clown:**
My bosom pals *(addressing the fleas)*, this is the end of the journey — for you. Prepare to meet thy death.

*(The mallet is produced, and a search is made for a smooth, hard place for the execution.)*

**Hobo Clown:**
It should be done on cement.

*(It is then discovered that one clown has a bald head. One at a time fleas are placed in position and the hammer wielded, and each body is tenderly placed in the coffin. "The Dead March" is heard. With heads uncovered and with due solemnity the clowns fall in behind the casket as the funeral procession moves off the floor. Clowns produce bright bandanna handkerchiefs for their lamentations. A "rooter" may be concealed in the handkerchief.)*

# #25 Doing the Impossible

**PROPS:**

A small hoop                              Some gym mats

**CHARACTERS:**
Two tumbling clowns

**ACTION:**
A tumbling act is in progress.
Music stops. Roll of drums.
One of the clowns steps forward and announces that he and his partner will perform a stunt that has required years of practice and that, as far as is known, has been performed by no other living person.
The stunt requires absolute silence. It is a double somersault without aid of springboard.
One clown assumes spotter position in center of mats.
Second clown prepares for the run.
Drum roll — clown runs fiercely down the mat, only to stop. Two clowns whisper.

**First Clown:**
*(Announces that they forgot "the hoop.")* A double somersault is in itself a rather simple feat, and in order to make it more difficult the somersault will be made through a hoop.

A small hoop is produced, which the spotter holds. It is paper-covered.
Again, the drums and the run. But as the clown lands on both feet preparatory for the leap, all the lights go out.
In the darkness the one clown smashes his fist through the paper covering the hoop as his companion dives into a forward roll.
Lights immediately flick back on as clown finishes his roll.
Both run to the front and take their bows.

# #26 Duck for the Oyster

**SCENE:**
The floor is cleared for a square dance.
Caller in costume takes his place at the "mike."
Caller plays a straight part.
Public-address music or pianist: "Rakes O'Mallow."

**CHARACTERS:**
Square-dance caller
Eight male clowns (four dressed as females)

**ACTION:**
Caller announces he is going to demonstrate how easy it is for anyone to learn square-dancing.
He calls for volunteers.
Eight young men run onto the floor attired for square-dancing. Four of them are dressed as girls.
They form a set and start clapping hands.
Caller assures the audience they have never danced before.
Caller proceeds to call as follows, the numbers here *(see description of actions listed after the call)* indicating suggested actions on the part of the dancers. Each action stops the dance. The caller goes up to the group, makes a brief explanation, and the dance starts over again. On each repeat, the dance is done correctly until the next new number comes along.

**CALL:**
All jump up and never come down. (1)
Grab your girl and roll her round. (2)
Now you're set remember the call;
      All together, center fall. (3)
Up once more and back to the wall. (4)
Head couples lead and circle four.

Duck for the oyster, duck. (5)
Now for the clam, now dig. (6)
Duck for the oyster, now the clam;
   Now the sardine, take a full can. (7)
Turn the tin can inside out;
   A dishrag turn, and everybody shout. (8)

## DESCRIPTION OF ACTION:

1. If dancers are under some suspended apparatus, such as high bar or rings, they jump up and hang on apparatus until music stops. Otherwise, girls jump into boys' arms.
2. Bear-hug girl, lift off feet, and turn once in place, or put girl on floor and give her a shove with foot to turn her over.
3. All fall flat *(prone fall)*.
4. Go as far backward as possible.
5. Duck as though boxing. One dancer produces a starfish, herring, lobster or bottle of shrimps and asks, "Will this do?"
6. Same as (5), but different article. Dancers can catch necks on opposite arms when ducking through.
7. All bump and huddle together, and a tin of sardines is proudly displayed.
8. Dancers get so horribly knotted and entangled that caller quits in disgust.

More music is heard, and dancers quickly find their partners to exit to a polka, conga or bunny hop.

# #27 Electric Rope

## PROPS:

Length of thick rope
Rubber egg
Table

Blown egg
Slapstick
Hat

## CHARACTERS:

Clown magician

Several other clowns

## ACTION:

Clown magician enters carrying the rope. He is followed by a number of curious clowns.

**Magician:**

All this way for the big magic show.

Clowns gather round table in center of floor. Magician takes the blown egg from his pocket and places it on the table. Egg is covered with a hat. Magician makes a few magic passes and hocus-pocus, and goes to one of the clowns who has concealed the rubber egg in his mouth.

Magician slaps this clown on the back, and the rubber egg drops into his hand. Magician swoops hat *(and egg still inside it)* off the table and puts the hat on his head.

The magician announces the feature attraction, "electrifying the rope." Two or three clowns are selected to serve as electric light poles and they are asked to take hold of the rope. The magician makes his magic passes in an effort to electrify the rope.

**Magician:**
Do you feel anything?

Clowns shake their heads, so it is apparent there are not enough poles. Other clowns are added.

**Magician:**
Do you feel anything now?

**Other Clowns:**
No.

The audience is now asked to help, and the rope is passed along to others.

**Another Clown:**
*(Finally)* Say, just what are you trying to do, anyway?

**Magician:**
I'm trying to see how many suckers I can get on the line at one time.

Magician bows. Clown picks up slapstick and hits magician on seat, and when magician jerks to a stand he is hit on the head *(where the egg is)* and the yolk is on him.

# #28 Fire! Fire!

**PROPS:**

| | |
|---|---|
| Frying pan | Candle |
| Match | Hot dog |
| Bucket or pail of water | Pail of confetti |

**CHARACTERS:**

| | |
|---|---|
| Hobo clown | Two firefighter clowns |
| Snooping clown | |

**ACTION:**
Hobo clown saunters onto the floor whistling to himself.

Selecting a spot near the center of the floor, he unslings the frying pan from his back and lights the candle, placing it on the floor.

He rummages through his pockets, turning out a lot of junk. Finally he is rewarded by finding a badly beaten-up wiener or hot dog.

Hot dog is placed in frying pan and cooked over fire *(candle)*. Clown smacks lips and rubs stomach in anticipation.

Another clown doing a bit of snooping discovers the scene.

**Snooping Clown:**
*(Cupping his hands)* Fire! Fire!

Two more clowns rush on *(wearing firefighters' helmets)* and carrying a pail between them. The contents *(water)* are swished over the fire, the hot dog and the hobo clown.

Clown firefighters exit, congratulating themselves.

Hobo sets up in business again. This time he is in front of audience *(girls preferred)*.

Routine is repeated. This time the pail is full of confetti, and the contents are thrown in the direction of the audience.

## #29 Flower Stunt

**PROPS:**
Two long-stemmed carnations, fresh and real (The stem of one is cut through about three inches from the flower.)

**ACTION:**
Clown enters carrying flowers and holding them so that both flowers appear to have full-length stems.

Business of smelling flowers, skipping about, etc. "Spring Music" could be supplied as background.

Clown decides to honor some sweet young things with the flowers and lays groundwork accordingly. Finally a young lady receives carnation No. 1 *(the uncut one)*.

Second lady gets the stem only when the presentation is made. Clown discovers mistake. Rushes back and exchanges flower for stem. Next, he wonders what to do with stem. Finally, he gives it, too, to the lady.

## #30 Fooled Again

**PROPS:**

| | |
|---|---|
| Stepladder | Long pole |
| Glass of water | |

**CHARACTERS:**

| | |
|---|---|
| Smart clown | Dumb clown |
| Two other clowns | Ringmaster |
| Accomplice | |

**ACTION:**

Smart clown enters, carrying a glass of water. He circles the gym, inspecting the ceiling or the underpart of the gallery.

Dumb clown trails first clown trying to guess what it is all about.

Smart clown explains that he can make the glass of water stick to the ceiling.

**Dumb Clown:**

Oh, yeah!

They bet.

Smart clown whistles, and two other clowns bring in the stepladder and the long pole.

Smart clown places ladder under previously selected spot, and climbing the ladder, he places the glass mouth-side-up against the ceiling. He then holds it in place with one end of the long stick.

He asks the dumb clown to hold the other end of the stick and to keep the glass in place while he descends, where he will say the magic words.

When smart clown gets down, he picks up stepladder and walks off, leaving dumb clown holding glass of water on ceiling above his head.

An accomplice whispers to the ringmaster, at the same time pointing to glass and then to floor. Ringmaster whispers in dumb clown's ear, pointing to glass and also to floor.

Other clowns sit down, the better to enjoy the dumb clown's perplexing situation.

Dumb clown is stuck for several minutes. He indicates that his neck is stiff, but no help is forthcoming. Dumb clown gets too weary to look at the ceiling.

Lights go out for a moment and an accomplice reaches through a trap door or over the edge of the gallery and removes the glass, leaving the stick braced against the ceiling.

Lights come on. There is no glass on the ceiling, but clown continues to hold pole in position until jeers and laughs put him wise. He slinks off with pole between his legs.

# #31 Handcuff Escape

**PROPS:**

A pair of handcuffs                     A screen

**CHARACTERS:**

Ringmaster                              Escapo

**ACTION:**

*(Screen is placed on the floor. The ringmaster makes a great speech about the famous escape artist procured at tremendous expense for this very special occasion.)*

**Ringmaster:**
This handcuff king has appeared before the crowned heads of Europe and the bald heads of America. Tonight he will thrill you with his famous handcuff escape — a feat that has baffled police for years. That is why he is here tonight. Ladies and gentlemen, I give you "Escapo," the magical escape artist.

*(Escapo may be dressed for the occasion, or straight clown costume will do. Escapo enters to a roll of drums or fanfare. He bows. He then produces a pair of handcuffs which he passes around for inspection. After due ceremony the ringmaster places the handcuffs on Escapo's wrists. Inspection is again invited, and Escapo promenades around showing wrists and handcuffs to the audience. Escapo is placed behind the screen. More continued drum rolls.)*

**Ringmaster:**
Ladies and gentlemen, in just 15 seconds, Escapo, the magnificent, will be free.

*(Ringmaster counts from 15 down to one, and on the last number he draws aside the screen, revealing Escapo still handcuffed. Ringmaster looks embarrassed.)*

**Ringmaster:**
Maybe Escapo needs a little more time.

*(Screen is replaced. Next number is announced. After each number the screen is removed to show Escapo more and more disheveled but still handcuffed. Escapo never does get out of the handcuffs — at least while the show is on.)*

# #32 Hide the Egg

**PROPS:**
One blown egg

**ACTION:**
Clowns form a circle around one clown who is "It."

Clowns produce an egg, which they pass or toss around the circle.

Clown in center closes his eyes. Egg is again passed around among clowns in the circle.

Finally, one clown holds the egg behind his back, and all circle players hold both hands behind their backs. Leader says, "Ready." And "It" opens his eyes. He tries to guess who has the egg, and points to his selection.

If he guesses right the two clowns change positions. If not, the game is repeated with the same "It."

On the fifth go-around, one of the circle clowns has a smart idea and indicates to all that he is hiding the egg in his pocket.

When the word *ready* is said, the clowns hold hands overhead. "It" walks around the circle trying to figure who has the egg.

He suddenly makes his decision and swats the pocket containing the egg.

The "goat" puts his hand in his pocket and makes appropriate faces as the others give him the raspberry.

# #33 "I Thought You Was Ossie"

## PROPS:
Cigar                                          Match

Public-address system

## CHARACTERS:
Voice 1                                        Clown 1

Voice 2                                        Clown 2

## ACTION:
*(This act is performed in pantomime by two clowns. Two different voices are heard over the P.A., with the clowns providing the appropriate action and, if desired, moving their mouths to synchronize with the spoken words. Those speaking the lines should not be seen by the audience. Two clowns enter from opposite sides and meet in the center.)*

**Voice 1:**

Well, well, well. Hello, Ossie! How are you, Ossie! My goodness, if it isn't good old Ossie. Haven't seen you for years. How's that cute little sister? Boy, this is like old times. Here, have a cigar.

**Clown 1:**

*(Simultaneously with Voice 1, grabs the reluctant hand of Clown 2. Clown 1 acts genuinely and enthusiastically pleased at coming across his old pal. He slaps him on the back. Rolls his eyes when he mentions the sister. Finally he puts a cigar in Clown 2's mouth.)*

**Voice 2:**

Bub-b-b-but —

**Clown 2:**

*(Indicates he doesn't recognize Clown 1 but is too shy to come right out and say so.)*

**Voice 1:**

Say, you are looking fine. A little fatter, perhaps. And a new suit. But I'd know you anywhere. Here, have a light.

**Clown 1:**
*(Simultaneously keeps up his enthusiasm. Looks Clown 2 up and down from head to toe and goes through motions indicating extra curves. Takes match and lights the cigar which is still in Clown 2's mouth.)*

**Voice 2:**
Bub-b-b-but —

**Voice 1:**
I'll bet you're the same old Ossie. Remember the fun we used to have in Chicago? Remember the time —

**Clown 1:**
*(While Voice 1 is talking, Clown 1 laughs as he recalls Chicago and doubles up to slap his knees after "Remember the time.")*

**Voice 2:**
But I was never in Chicago and my name is not Ossie. You've mistaken me for someone else.

**Clown 2:**
*(Simultaneously with Voice 2, first puts hands on chest — "not Ossie." Throws hands wide apart on "You've mistaken me . . . " and holds the pose.)*

**Voice 1:**
You're not Ossie? Excuse me! I'm very sorry.

**Clown 1:**
*(Clown 1 takes cigar out of Clown 2's mouth and exits smoking it, leaving Clown 2 standing in perplexed amazement. Blackout.)*

## #34 It's in the Bag

**PROPS:**

| | |
|---|---|
| Hot water bag | Funnel |
| Pitcher of water | |

**CHARACTERS:**

| | |
|---|---|
| Two smart clowns | Rube clown |
| Acrobatic clown | |

**ACTION:**

Two smart clowns escort a visiting rube clown around the gym. The rube is shown various points of interest. He is introduced to people in the audience. Finally, his attention is directed to a third clown who is swinging high on the rings.

While the rube gazes intently toward the swinging clown, one of the smart ones produces a large funnel from behind his back and inserts it under the belt of the rube's pants.

The second smart clown produces a pitcher of water and proceeds to pour the contents down the funnel.

In the meantime the first smart clown keeps pointing at the swinging clown and successfully diverts the rube's attention from the monkey business at hand.

The funnel, of course, was inserted in the neck of the hot water bag which was fastened inside the rube's trousers.

When there is no water left in the pitcher, the rube produces the bag and exits triumphantly.

The smart clowns faint, and the rube returns and revives them by sprinkling them with the contents of the bag.

# #35 King's Pond

**PROPS:**

Drinking glass of water          Toy dagger

**CHARACTERS:**

Small Clown 1          Small Clown 2
Tall Clown

**ACTION:**

*(Two small clowns and one large clown take the floor.)*

**Small Clown 1:**

I've got a swell game, but we must have a king. *(Looks around.)*

**Tall Clown:**

Well, I'm the biggest; I'll be king.

*(The small clowns clap hands in glee and set the king on the floor. He could be crowned.)*

**Tall Clown:**

How do you play this game?

**Small Clown 1:**

You're the king and so you own the royal pond. Here's the pond. *(He spreads the king's legs and the other small clown pours a glassful of water on the floor between the king's legs.)*

**Tall Clown:**

Now what? *(Looks bewildered.)*

**Small Clown 2:**

You're a jealous king, and you won't let anyone play in your pond, so with this dagger *(other small clown hands dagger to king)* you try to stab anyone trying to get into your pond.

**Tall Clown:**
*(Takes the dagger, and flourishing it menacingly, he shouts:)* Well, let's
see you knaves get my pond.

**Small Clowns:**
*(Go into a huddle, bend over with laughter. They approach the king and
say together:)* We don't want your old pond; you can have it.

*(They each grab a king's ankle and pull him through his pond, and then
run off.)*

# #36 Last Court of Appeal

**PROPS:**

Soft-drink case                              Stepladder

**CHARACTERS:**

Clown                                        Police officer

**ACTION:**

*(Clown enters carrying a soft-drink case, such as used on Coca-Cola
delivery trucks. Clown walks around floor in clockwise direction until he
bumps into police officer going the other way.)*

**Officer:**
What have you got there?

**Clown:**
I've got a case.

**Officer:**
That I can see. Where are you taking it?

**Clown:**
I'm taking it to court.

*(Police officer swings billy at clown, who continues his circuit of the floor.
Another minute and clown is back again, going the other way. This time,
in addition to the case, he has a stepladder. He bumps into the police officer
again.)*

**Police Officer:**
What have you got there?

**Clown:**
I've got a case.

**Police Officer:**
Where are you taking it?

**Clown:**
I'm taking it to a higher court.

*(Police officer chases clown off. Clown drops ladder, and police officer stumbles over it. Clown comes out and offers him a drink of pop, which shoots off in police officer's face. Clown had earlier removed cap, shaken up bottle, and kept thumb over opening.)*

# #37 Mind-Reader

**PROPS:**
Pencil and paper

**ACTION:**
*(One clown wears a turban — rolled towel — and a loose, flowing gown. Second clown gives him the once-over and asks him what he is supposed to be. The first clown is both haughty and offended.)*

**First Clown:**
Me, I'm a mind-reader. *(The other gives him a dirty laugh and challenges him to prove it.)*

**Second Clown:**
How about reading my mind?

**First Clown:**
I can't read blank verse.

**Second Clown:**
That is just because you wouldn't know an intelligent mind if you met one. And I don't believe you're a mind-reader.

**First Clown:**
Very well, just to prove how foolish you are, I'll read your alleged mind. You write anything you want on a piece of paper and I'll tell you what's on it.

**Second Clown:**
If I write something on a piece of paper you'll tell me what's on it?

**First Clown:**
That's right.

*(Mind-reader turns his back. Other clown writes. The paper is folded, and the mind-reader is challenged. The mind-reader goes into deep thought. The other clown looks smug. Mind-reader says the writing is so bad he is having trouble and suggests the other clown stand on the paper. This is done.)*

**Second Clown:**
*(Fires the question:)* Well, what's on the paper?

**First Clown:**
*(On his way out)* Nothing but a darn fool.

## #38 No! No! A Thousand Times No!

**PROPS:**
Stetson hat and lady's broadbrimmed bonnet
Song sheet of the title above

**SETTING:**
This is a solo requiring some voice ability.
It may be presented by a clown or eccentric and may be performed as an
    encore or as a feature of a glee club program.

**ACTION:**
The singer presents the song, acting out the various parts as follows, with
    the appropriate variations in voice.

**Villain:**
Pulls down brim of Stetson.
Holds blackened index finger below nose to represent a mustache.
Scowls.
Hunches shoulders and rounds back.

**Hero:**
Turns brim of hat upward.
Smiles à la Pepsodent.

**Heroine:**
Exchanges Stetson for bonnet which has been held behind back.
Sings in high falsetto.
Holds imaginary skirt and moves coyly about.

*(Breaks into regular voice, saying:)* This corset is killing me.

## #39 Not So Bright

**PROPS:**
A candle

**CHARACTERS:**
Several clowns                                    Clown police officer

**ACTION:**
Lights go out.
Clown rushes in with a candle. He tells everyone not to worry, lights will
   be on in a minute.
Other clowns follow in.
Lights come on. Clowns act pleased. Can't decide what to do with candle.
Decide to blow it out. Clown with candle blows at it out of the side of his
   mouth. He can't blow it out.
All others try to blow out candle. All fail because each blows out of a dif-
   ferent corner of his mouth.
Clown police officer, who has remained aloof, is called upon.
He blows it out first time.
Clowns are amazed.

**All Clowns:**
*(Except officer)* How did you do it?

**Police Officer:**
That shows you the value of a college education.

Police officer puffs out his chest. Other clowns chase him off.

## #40 Pop Goes the Weasel

**ACTION:**
Following an exhibition of square-dancing, eight clowns take the floor
   for "Pop Goes the Weasel."
Four are men; four are ladies. The music is played or piped in, and a caller
   calls. *(The calls are listed first, and then the corresponding actions.)*

**CALL:**
Head couple out to the right and do not make a blunder. (1)
Join your hands and circle four and pop that couple under. (2)
On to the next and balance there and do not make a blunder. (3)
Join your hands and circle four and pop that couple under. (4)
On to the last and balance there and do not make a blunder. (5)
Join your hands and circle a half; pop those weasels under. (6)
Allemande left the corners all, right hand to your partner; (7)
Grand chain all. (8)
All around the chicken house door the monkey chased the weasel.
The monkey stopped to scratch a flea, pop went the weasel.
All swing out when you come home and do not make a blunder. (9)
Swing your honey, swing some more; pop goes the weasel.

**DESCRIPTION OF ACTION:**
   1. First couple moves out to face second couple. The four join hands.
   2. These four circle halfway round to the left. Couple two makes an
      arch and couple one goes under, getting a kick as it goes through.

3. Couple one, now in the center, moves on to face couple three. For a balance, the four paddy-cake opposite.

4. Repeat (2).

5. & 6. Repeat (3) and (4) but with last couple.

7. This is a regular "allemande left." It is called, not sung.

8. This is regular grand chain or grand right and left.

9. For the swing, partners take dancing positions, but standing wide of each other and leaning in, they run around furiously.

The dance is repeated once only for the second couple.

After the "allemande left" the dancers break formation and do not do the grand right and left, although the caller calls it. Instead, the dancers rush to the sides of the gym where they take partners from the audience. Taking them by both hands, they pull them to their feet, turn them around twice, and then leave them in time to scurry back to place and shout with the caller as they huddle, *"Pop goes the weasel!"*

***(For any of the following six acts, 41a to 41f, inclusive, use good singers in costume.)***

# #41a Grand Opera

Opera singer and clown.

Spotlights on each; other lights out.

Opera is sung as clown goes through contortions of agony.

Clown shoots singer, who spits out bullet. Two more shots — two more pellets out.

Clown goes offstage and returns with small cannon. Singer runs for life.

# #41b Inverted Singers

Singers perform from behind a curtain with only their heads showing.

After their first song it is announced that they are acrobats as well and will sing their second number standing on their heads.

They stoop down, put shoes upside down on their hands, and hold these just above the curtain.

A careless stagehand gives the show away by raising and/or lowering the curtain.

# #41c Old Oaken Bucket

**PROPS:**

Draped table

Bucket

Wire paper basket

**CHARACTERS:**

Clown 1

Clown 3

Clown 2

Clown 4

**ACTION:**

*(Musical accompaniment optional.)*

A clown quartet comes onto the floor and sings a chorus of "The Old Oaken Bucket."

"The old oaken bucket, the ironbound bucket,
The moss-covered *bucket* that hung in the well."

On the italicized word, Clown 1 goes off-key. There is general consternation, and that party sneaks off in hangdog fashion.

The trio starts again, but Clown 2 misses on the same word. He leaves.

A duet is now attempted, but Clown 3 finishes on the same word.

Bravely, the last clown commences his solo. When he comes to the second line, dozens of voices shout, according to previous instruction, "Aw, sit down!", and rolled or crumpled napkins are thrown at the singer.

Clown 4 ducks under the table as the barrage hits him, but he comes up singing correctly the last part of the line with a wire paper basket on top of his head and an old oaken bucket in his hand. He swings the bucket jauntily as he walks off.

# #41d Serenade

A large quarter moon is built from plywood. It is illuminated from a rear spotlight.

A lady singer sits in the moon, and as the song opens, the moon is behind a fence. Gradually the moon rises, and the lady in the moon is serenaded by one or more singers.

A black cat can appear on the fence and meow at appropriate intervals.

# #41e Sing a Song Backward

After a regular number it is announced that is is relatively simple to sing a song the way it is written, but extremely difficult to sing a song backward.

That will now be demonstrated.

Singers turn backs to audience and sing their next song. Finish with a low bow.

# #41f Suicide Quartet

They sing a well-known ballad, on one note of which each in turn goes off-key.

**First Miscue:**
Leader takes offender offstage, and a shot is heard. The leader returns alone. Song is started again with misgivings.

**Second Miscue:**
Leader takes offender off, and a scream is heard. Leader returns, wiping large knife with a cloth.

**Third Miscue:**
Heavy dull sound. Leader returns, carrying a large mallet.

**Fourth Miscue:**
The leader himself. He retires with appropriate gestures, and a shot is heard. No one returns.

# #42 Tug of War

**PROPS:**
One long length of heavy rope

**ACTION:**
This stunt is performed where there is a stage with wings or a gym with doors on opposite sides.

A clown dressed as a strong man enters through one door pulling on a long length of rope. He just gets nicely in when he is jerked onto the seat of his pants. He regains his footing, and facing the door through which he entered, he acts as though he were pulling against a team of horses.

After much straining, and at times losing ground, the clown finally tugs his way across the floor and disappears through the other door. Here a property man takes over that end of the rope, and meanwhile, of course, the other end of the rope is likewise controlled by a property man.

The property men, now at both ends of the rope, keep it seesawing back and forth as the clown makes his way by basement, backstage or halls until he eventually takes over the other end of the rope.

The rope continues to be pulled in the one general direction until the same
clown again appears with even greater straining and hauling.
Halfway across, the clown falls flat on his face and is dragged off.

# #43 The Wonderful Dollar

**PROPS:**
A one-dollar bill

**CHARACTERS:**
First clown                    Second clown
Third clown

**ACTION:**
*(First clown walks to the center of the floor, followed by second clown
about 10 paces back. They are followed by third clown whose entrance
is delayed for timing purposes. First clown stoops down and picks up a
dollar bill. He feels pretty good about his find.)*

**Second Clown:**
*(Tapping first clown on the shoulder)* How about the two dollars you owe
me?

**First Clown:**
All right, here's a dollar on account.

*(Second clown pockets bill. Second clown is tapped on shoulder by
third clown.)*

**Third Clown:**
How about the two dollars you owe me?

**Second Clown:**
OK, here's a dollar on account.

**Third Clown:**
*(To first clown)* Remember the two dollars I borrowed from you? Well,
here's a dollar on account.

*(First clown has his dollar back.)*

**First Clown:**
*(To second clown)* I still owe you a dollar, don't I? Well, here it is, and
we're all fair and square.

**Third Clown:**
*(To second clown)* Now that you've got a dollar you might as well pay
me off. *(Bill is passed over.)* And now we're all square.

**First Clown:**
*(To third clown)* And you still owe me a dollar.

**Third Clown:**
And I always pay my debts. Here you are.

*(Clowns walk off in single file.)*

**First Clown:**
*(Figuring aloud)* I found a dollar, paid a two-dollar debt, and still have a
    dollar. Boy, that's high financing!

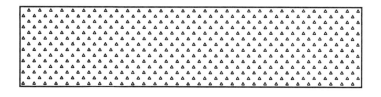

## CHAPTER 6

# Clown Acts with Special Equipment

# #44 Abused Car Lot

**PROPS:**
A youngster's toy automobile
A couple of floodlights and poles
Sign: HONEST A-1 GUARANTEED UNCONDITIONED CARS
Two chairs
Vacuum cleaner
Electric fan

**SCENE:**
Poles, lights, sign and chair are arranged to represent a sales office or
used-car lot. The car is the center of attraction.

**CHARACTERS:**
Two clown salesmen
One blind customer (a clown policeman wearing a regular clown suit
over his policeman's uniform.) He has a small valise.

**ACTION:**
*(Salesmen are sitting down reading newspapers when blind man comes
tapping his way in with a white cane. Blind man stops in front.)*

**Blind Man:**
Is this the corner of Brad and Nail? *(He uses names of local streets. Eager
salesmen tell him it is.)* Well, I'm looking for —

**Salesmen:**
*(Shouting)* Say no more. You've come to the right spot.

*(Salesmen give the customer the works. Very high-pressure. They have
him feel the hood and other parts by lifting the car to the respective heights.)*

**Salesman 1:**
Real steel *(striking the metal with his knuckles)*.

*(A trial run is proposed. Blind man is seated in car. Blind man protests he
can't drive.)*

**Salesman 2:**
Don't worry. This car practically drives itself.

*(Motor — vacuum cleaner — is turned on. Comments on condition of motor.)*

**Salesman 1:**
And the mileage. Uses hardly any gas.

*(Car is put in motion. One salesman pushes in the back and talks all the time. The other walks backward in front of the car with an electric fan directed at the driver, who acts very excited over the speed. Ride completed, the blind man is helped out.)*

**Blind Man:**
If that car is all you say it is, I'll take it.

*(Salesmen rub hands and ask if customer has checkbook with him.)*

**Blind Man:**
Yes, I have a pen in my inside coat pocket and a checkbook in my inside
pants pocket.

*(Blind man fumbles.)*

**Salesmen:**
We'll help you.

*(They strip blind man, revealing police uniform, as the police officer opens valise to don his police cap and billy, with which he chases salesmen.)*

# #45 The Artist

**PROPS:**
Artist's smock and easel
A canvas on frame and stand bearing a previously painted picture or a
colored one from Sunday paper
Sign: YOUR PORTRAIT PAINTED — $100

**ACTION:**
Sign is placed or carried about by clown assistant.
Artist, very affected, comes in carrying easel.
Clown customer comes in. He sees sign and contracts for picture, paying
money.
The canvas is set up so that the audience cannot see the working side.
Customer poses — and how he poses!
The artist goes to work. He adjusts poses, and very carelessly, his wet
brush smears the clown.
As work progresses the artist shows satisfaction, and the clown's head and
chest swell with pride. *(Another act can go on during the painting.)*

Artist steps back once in a while to admire his work. Finally, the artist turns the canvas so that the customer and the audience can see what he has accomplished: a mule's head.

Customer chases artist.

# #46 At Ptomaine Tommy's

## PROPS:
Two knock-down tables parallel and six feet apart
Pots, pans and wash basin half-full of water
Three eggs: one rubber, one china, one real
Two brooms
Restaurant stools or facsimiles
Bicycle pump or squirt gun

## SCENE:
A restaurant, "Ptomaine Tommy's"

## CHARACTERS:
One clown cook                    One clown customer

## ACTION:
Cook enters and busies himself stirring soup in wash basin with large ladle, or with golf club.

Customer seats himself. Goes to order but can't speak.

Cook slaps him on back, and a rubber egg bounces on table.

Cook catches it and throws it in soup.

Business of sprinkling pepper in soup.

Both sneeze terrifically, covering noise-makers with handkerchiefs.

**Customer:**
What are you cooking?

**Cook:**
Makin' soup. Have some?

Cook loads bicycle pump with soup and squirts customer in face.

**Customer:**
I want a fresh, fried egg. I mean I want a fried egg — fresh.

Cooks tries to break china egg. Fresh egg is produced, and cook cracks it on top of customer's head. Cook holds egg high above the frying pan and starts to open shell. Customer moves pan, cook hollers, customer catches egg yolk in his hand.

The chase.

Customer jumps on top of cook's table, and cook crawls underneath. Customer washes his hands in the soup. Cook gives customer another shot of soup.

Customer jumps down on far side of cook's table. Both get back on top of opposite tables, picking up brooms en route. They take turns swinging brooms at each other, but low enough for a skipping routine. Cook falls off his table and rolls under other. Business of trying to swat cook. Cook raises the table on his back creating a teeter-totter which customer attempts to balance. Customer slides off and chases cook to exit. *(Hand-balancing routines are done on table-tops.)*

# #47 At the Optometrist's

**PROPS:**
Desk and desk lamp
Two chairs
Sign: DR. I.M. BLIND — OPTOMETRIST
Some official-looking instruments
An easel holding a number of rolled window blinds
Pair of large horn-rimmed glasses
White jacket

**ACTION:**
Optometrist is at desk wearing his white jacket.
Clown patient enters wearing large glasses.
Doctor and patient exchange greetings. Patient sits in chair facing doctor. Business of looking in eyes. Doctor decides to give eye-chart test and has patient face the easel.
The first window shade is pulled down to expose a lot of jumbled letters, but so fine no one could read them.
Patient shakes his head, after considerable straining.
Another shade is used. This time the letters are slightly larger, but again the patient shakes his head.
This is repeated several times until the letters are so large that everyone in the hall can see them plainly.

**Doctor:**
*(In desperation)* Do you mean to say you can't even see these letters?

**Patient:**
Certainly, I can see the letters, but I can't pronounce the words. *(Blackout.)*

# #48 Auto Polo

**PROPS:**
Six kiddy cars
Six croquet mallets
Six football helmets

Sets of hockey goals
One light plastic ball (30-inch circumference)

**ACTION:**

There are two clown polo teams, three to a side, mounted on kiddie cars.

Players wear football helmets, three blue, three red. Each player has a croquet mallet; three are blue, three red.

The referee or ringmaster lines up the teams at the goal lines where the hockey nets have been placed, and starts the game by tossing the ball onto the center of the floor.

The object of the game is, first, to drive the ball into the audience as frequently as possible and to get the crowd to assist and root for the team of their choosing; and second, to score a goal.

When a goal is scored the scorer is shouldered by his two teammates and paraded off the floor.

# #49 The Beany Players

**PROPS:**

A live microphone, turntable and record (see Action)
Cowbell
Four plumber's helpers (sink vacuum pumps)
Four dishpans of water and assorted objects such as bean bags
Four tin pie plates, pea shooters and peas
Guns with blank cartridges, inflated balloon, tin bank

**ACTION:**

*(A clown radio announcer and five clown actors gather round the microphone. The announcer strikes the cowbell, and then the five clowns sing, one letter each, **H, E, L, L**. The fifth clown has gone to sleep and on being nudged, wakes up to sing **O**.)*

**Announcer:**

It is now my pleasure to bring you that *card* of all *cards*, that *jack* of foolishness, that *ace* of fun; the man who plays *deuce* with the ladies — *Jack Beany.*

**Jack:**

Hello again; this is Jack Beany with our peppy Saturday night program. Say, Don, did you hear the one about the *deaf* sheep rancher? He watched over his sheep and *herd*. *(All laugh uproariously.)*

**Announcer:**

Boy, that's a good one. Where did you get it?

**Jack:**

I don't know. *(Turning to first clown)* Where did I get it? *(Clowns repeat this last line from one to the other.)*

**Announcer:**
Ladies and gentlemen, Jack Beany, assisted by Soy Beany, Navy Beany, String Beany *(the tallest)* and "Has" Beany, will now present a classic of the screen, *Buck Beany Rides Again. (Clowns bow as introduced.)* The curtain rises and our scene opens. The Beany brothers are being pursued by a tribe of wild Indians.

*(Clowns thump vacuum pumps on the floor and vibrate hands, from time to time, over their mouths as they yell like Indians.)*

**Announcer:**
The Beany brothers come to a river and dive in, one after the other.

*(Drop bean bags into dishpans of water. Substitute a piece of metal for the fourth bean bag.)*

**Announcer:**
"Has" Beany has been; he doesn't come up. There come the others to the surface. *(Clowns blow bubbles in pans of water as their names are called.)* There's Jack. And Navy and Soy. *(Pause)* Sorry, we had to get rid of String before this strung out too far.
The Indians begin to shoot. *(Fire blank cartridges and blow peas out of pea shooters against empty pie plates. Scream.)* Soy Beany says, "Soy long." *(Balloon bursts.)* And there goes our Navy. Only Jack is left. *(Shake tin bank containing coppers.)*
Tune in next week for another episode with the Beany players. Meanwhile, here is our quartet to close off. *(Some jingle is played over P.A., and clowns mouth the words.)*

# #50 The Booking Agency

**PROPS:**
Desk
Telephone book
Note pad
Pencil
Telephone
Talk-back system
Sign: BOOKING AGENCY — VAUDEVILLE TALENT WANTED

**ACTION:**
*(A "straight" character enters and sits at the desk on which are sign, telephone, book and pad. The talk-back system allows the person at the desk to carry on a conversation with someone offstage. Clowns drift in one at a time, and spotting the sign, they apply for a job. Each clown has some specialty such as tumbling, hand-balancing, juggling, singing. After each little act the agent says, "No, I'm looking for something different." Last clown exits. The telephone rings:)*

**Agent:**
Hello.

**Voice:**
Hello, is this the Vaudeville Booking Agency?

**Agent:**
Yes, what can I do for you?

**Voice:**
I've got something different that you really ought to see.

**Agent:**
Can you tell me what it is over the phone?

**Voice:**
Well, it's a dog that talks.

**Agent:**
*(Excitedly)* What's that? Say, who's speaking?

**Voice:**
Oh, I forgot to tell you. I'm the dog. *(Lights)*

# #51 Buggy Marathon

**PROPS:**

Stage money
Starting gun
Magnifying glass
A long elastic cord (black)

Piece of chalk
Bandanna handkerchief
Bellows or fan

**ACTION:**

Two clowns scratch themselves as though inhabited. Each clown discovers the offender. Apparently the fleas are so large and strong as to be admired at arm's length by the clowns.

It is decided to hold a race, and a course is marked off with the chalk.

Each wants to bet on his flea *(stage money)* and a third clown is called in to hold the bets. *(While the third clown is doing this, he ties one end of the elastic cord around the roll of money.)*

Clowns kneel at starting mark. A fourth clown fires the starting gun, and the race is on.

Much cheering and excitement. One bug goes the wrong way, but is waved back on the course with the bandanna handkerchief.

The other bug gets way ahead and stops. No amount of urging moves it. Clown gets out magnifying glass to see what is wrong. The other clown asks him what the trouble is and gets the reply, "When you gotta go, you gotta go."

The other clown meantime has been helping his bug along with a bellows which he had up his pant leg. Eventually, one bug crosses the finish line.

The winner, rubbing his hands in anticipation of his winnings, looks for the holder of the bets, who has edged toward the exit.

Both bettors let out a holler and capture the bet-holder before he can get away. They take the money and return with it to the middle of the floor.

When they arrive there the money is whisked back to the third clown by means of the elastic cord, and he quickly does a disappearing act, chased by the others.

# #52 Calling Mr. Schnittzlebaum

**PROPS:**
Four to six potted plants (palm or rubber), from very small to very large
A half-dozen bananas

**ACTION:**
A clown enters, carrying a very small potted plant.

He circles the floor, calling "Parcel for Mr. Schnittzlebaum, parcel for Mr. Schnittzlebaum."

Of course no one answers to the name, and the clown leaves the floor with the plant.

After the next act the same clown re-enters and repeats his performance. However, the plant has grown noticeably larger.

This routine is repeated between acts until finally the clown staggers in under the weight of a huge plant. He can scarcely find the breath or energy to call, "Parcel for Mr. Schnittzlebaum."

The clown is soon exhausted and sits down to rest under the "shade" of the plant.

Clown reaches up into the leaves and pulls off a banana which he eats.

All the other clowns, who have seated themselves among the audience, yell in unison: *"Did you say Schnittzlebaum?"*

These clowns descend en masse on the single clown, help themselves to bananas, and exit eating same.

# #53 Corn Doctor

**PROPS:**

| | |
|---|---|
| Ear of corn | Operating table |
| Hypodermic needle (clown size) | Pair of fire tongs |
| Bandages | Pair of crutches |
| Tweezer | Pliers |

71

Popcorn and popper

**ACTION:**

Clown doctor sets up his operating table in the middle of the room.

Clown suffering from a very bad corn enters on crutches. *(One foot is heavily wrapped with bandages. An added effect is to have a red cellophane window in the bandages with a flash bulb attached to concealed batteries. Corn lights up.)*

The subject groans with pain, especially if another clown gets anywhere near him. Of course, these extra clowns are careless and drop articles very close to the sore foot.

Doctor gets subject face-down on table.

Running his hands up and down the patient's back, the doctor asks, "Which toe did you say it was?"

Subject sits up and doctor prepares to operate.

Local injection is given with hypodermic needle. Doctor smells foot and passes out. Doctor revives when patient gives him needle in trousers.

Tweezers — too small.

Pliers — too small.

Fire tongs — just right. Assistants hold patient, and doctor extracts ear of corn.

Doctor is chased off by patient. *(Patient returns with hopper filled with popped corn which he distributes to children. "Have some on me!")*

# #54 Cracker Swat

**PROPS:**

Two swatters
Soda biscuits or crackers
Two colors of ribbons
Comb (with most teeth missing)
Some hairbrushes (one has a trick handle)
A white, tame mouse
Miscellany of small articles — fake frogs, beetles, and the like
Two wigs

**ACTION:**

Two clowns wear wigs. A couple of crackers sit on top of wigs, fastened in place by ribbon. Clowns are distinguished by contrasting ribbon colors.

The ringmaster calls the clowns to the center of the floor where he presents each with a swatter and announces that the cracker king will be the one who first breaks the crackers on top of the other.

The duel commences and continues until a cracker is smashed. Referee congratulates the winner, giving him a box of crackers *(the balance)*.

The defeated clown sits down and woefully scratches the crumbs from the wig, eating the crumbs as he does.

Other clowns now come to his rescue with comb and brushes. Since the wig has been planted with the miscellaneous objects mentioned *(or the articles may be palmed by assisting clowns),* there is considerable amusement over the ridiculous articles removed.

One brush has a trick handle in which a white mouse is hidden. It is released to make it appear as though found in the hair.

Clowns exit, dangling mouse by tail. On the way, they make sure to pass by a few girls.

# #55 Cross-Eyed Clowns

**PROPS:**
A bench
Cigar, matches
Two pairs of goggles with cross-eyes painted on glass, but with a small, clear aperture that permits seeing

**ACTION:**
Two clowns *(wearing goggles)* enter and circle the gym in opposite directions, and meet in front of bench.

They go to shake hands but miss.

Both start to sit down but crisscross in so doing, one sliding across other's lap.

One attempts to cross his leg but crosses with other clown's leg.

One reaches in other's pocket and extracts a cigar. Second clown takes match out of first clown's pocket, strikes it on other's foot and eventually lights cigar.

One complains of tired feet and takes off other's shoes.

One sneezes and blows other's nose with handkerchief.

They get up to go, point in directions away from each other, then proceed to bump into each other. Both do backward rolls to stand and zigzag off the floor.

# #56 Dirty Work

**PROPS:**
Two garbage can lids made into shields
Two long wooden fencing foils, one end of each foil being covered with white cotton waste in the shape and size of a volleyball.
Tin loving cup
Bar of soap
Quantity of lampblack

**ACTION:**
Two clowns enter the arena. They are dressed in ragged trousers and are

stripped to the waist. Hair is held in place by caps made from the tops
of ladies' stockings tied in a knot.

Clowns carry spears or foils, as indicated, and shields.

The waste on the ends of the foils has been liberally treated with lampblack, and the object of the contest is to blacken one's opponent.

The bout is run in three rounds.

At the end of the third round the ringmaster calls on two or three people
to select the winner.

The winner is presented with the tin loving cup. The consolation prize is
a bar of soap.

## #57 Dog & Hoop

**PROPS:**
A youngster's play hoop or a barrel hoop
A toy stuffed dog

**ACTION:**
Clown brings out dog and hoop.

He pantomimes that dog will jump through hoop.

Several attempts are made but the dog does not budge.

Another clown comes in and is curious.

First clown asks second to hold hoop. He entices dog by offering tidbits
on opposite side of hoop.

He even gives the dog a little boost from the rear, but nothing happens.

Second clown gets an idea. He asks first clown to hold the hoop, and
he moves dog and hoop near the audience so that with a long jump
the dog would end up in the crowd.

When the dog is properly lined up, the first clown turns his head momentarily away, and the second clown boots dog through hoop into the
audience.

This can be repeated later in the program and at another location on
the floor.

## #58 Egg Magic

**PROPS:**
A folding screen
A rubber egg
A magician's table on which are sundry articles and a basket of eggs,
including a rubber one
Glass of water

**ACTION:**
Ringmaster announces "Blackrock, the great magician."

Stagehands set table in position where all can see. The screen is placed as a backdrop.

Magician may do one or two real stunts. He then requests an assistant. *(This may be a clown.)*

Magician explains that he intends to pass an egg through a very narrow aperture. He asks clown to stand behind the screen and put two fingers through one of the slits. Clown does so, and magician puts the egg between these two fingers.

Ringmaster reminds magician that they want no mess on the floor, because the building superintendent is present.

Magician says he forgot to bring a glass of water, which is necessary to the success of the act. He leaves. There is an embarrassing wait. *(Another act could go on.)*

Clown behind screen does zany antics but hangs on to egg.

Finally, magician returns with glass of water. He announces he will first cause the contents of the glass to disappear.

He drinks water. Takes egg from clown's hand, bounces it on the floor, pushes it through slit to clown.

Clown runs from behind screen and throws egg at magician heading for exit.

Clown may pick real egg out of basket and drop it as though expecting to catch it on the bounce.

# #59 Egg Toss

**PROPS:**
Basket of eggs, including two china eggs, or two hard-boiled
Four aprons
Two sets of salt and pepper shakers

**ACTION:**
Ringmaster asks for four volunteers for a contest. Four clowns volunteer.

Assistant brings out the aprons, which are tied around the clowns. It can be announced that this is to protect their costumes.

The basket of eggs is brought out and given to the ringmaster, who explains that the contest is a game of catch between two teams of two each. The idea is to see who can throw the egg the farthest and still keep the egg intact.

Ringmaster demonstrates with one of the clowns. They face each other in center of floor one pace apart. Egg is tossed by ringmaster to his codemonstrator. Egg is caught. Both take one step away from each other. Egg is tossed again. It is explained that with each successful catch the distance becomes greater. Ringmaster obtains egg.

Clowns are paired off one pace apart. Ringmaster tosses egg *(hard-boiled)* to Clown 1 of pair 1. He tosses real egg to Clown 2 of pair 2, who is busy showing off apron to audience. Result — egg goes over his

shoulder and smashes on floor. Second egg is tossed to him — this
time a hard-boiled one.

Contest starts, and clowns should be practiced catchers and throwers.
Under the direction of the ringmaster, they throw when instructed and
keep backing up until standing in bleachers or among spectators, much
to the consternation of the latter.

On a signal the hard-boiled eggs are thrown to two "pals" in the audience
who take out salt and pepper shakers and eat the eggs.

# #60 Family Portrait

## PROPS:
Clown camera which has old auto horn for bulb, and black cloth for light
hood attached to rear
A birdie on a stick
Three chairs (two kindergarten-size)

## CHARACTERS:
Clown photographer
Clown parents with two youngsters, Pa in a derby hat, and Ma with a
flowing black skirt

## ACTION:
Photographer busies himself setting up camera and placing chairs for a
family photo. Two small chairs are set in front and the other chair
at the rear.

The family arrives and is graciously received by the photographer. Mother
is seated in the large chair and father stands beside her, hat in hand.
The youngsters sit on the small seats.

Camera man goes about his business as the youngsters act up, making
faces, etc. One youngster sniffles, and mother blows his nose with a
hanky as the photographer accidentally squeezes the horn bulb.

Youngsters chase each other around the set. They are caught and soundly
spanked and reseated. They cry and try to smile through their tears at
the camera. Photographer waves birdie and comes forward to make
final adjustments.

Ma thinks she should see through the lens what the group looks like. She
lifts the camera cloth and continues to peer, while holding a bent-over
position.

Photographer, who has not noted Ma's absence, returns to take the
picture. He continues to look at the group, motioning them to hold
everything, and by mistake he lifts Ma's dress instead of the camera cloth.

There is much shouting and excitement from the family.

The horn toots several times, and Pa chases photographer off, followed
by the kids. Ma holds position. Pa comes back and removes Ma.

# #61 Fashion Show

**PROPS:**
Costumes as suggested below

**ACTION:**
The costumes are burlesque, but the action is serious. Music is piped in on the P.A. system.
A roll of carpet or canvas may be run out for the mannequins.
A fashion expert points out the features of each exhibit.
Mannequins are clowns.

1875 — Long, old-fashioned dress with bustle. Umbrella.
1900 — Long, flowing dress. Large picture hat, veil and muff
1925 — Short skirt, rolled stockings, much rouge, cigarette in holder, hat pulled down about ears.
1950 — Slim, tight-fitting evening dress.
1960 — Strapless bathing suit.
1986 — Appears in barrel marked "Censored."

Note: The bustle above may be a small boy covered with material matching the dress. Occasionally he gets separated from the main body of the costume.

# #62 Ferdinand

**PROPS:**
A bull (two boys or men) in costume
A toreador, in costume, and with a foil
P.A. music as indicated
Colored hankies or clothes as indicated

**ACTION:**
Ringmaster announces that at great expense they have procured one of the world's fiercest bulls and, direct from Spain, Señor Barbecue, renowned toreador. *(Selected music from **Carmen** is heard over P.A.)*
"Allow me to introduce, ladies and gentlemen, the one and only Señor Barbecue." The señor enters. "And now — please do not panic — ladies and gentlemen, I give you Ferdinand."
In contrast to the swaggering toreador, Ferdinand makes a bashful entry, peeking from behind curtains at entrance.
Toreador waves his frock, and Ferdinand takes a few skidding steps forward and then stops to scratch himself. One rear foot rubs opposite leg.
Señor Barbecue tries again. Ferdinand goes up to him, turns his back, and kicks up his heels in a can-can salute.
Polka music is heard. Ferdinand shows interest.

The bull performs to the polka music *(football or college song will do)* the dance called the "Dinkey One-Step."

## THE DINKEY:

Point left foot forward. Hold two counts.
Point same foot to the rear. Hold two counts.
Walk forward four steps, left, right, left, right. Repeat all.
Touch left foot lightly to left. Close left foot to right.
Same with right foot to right.
Step on left foot to left side. Swing right foot behind left.
Same opposite.
Eight steps forward, turning once around.
Toreador now gets into the dance, holding Ferdinand's horns as he would a dancing partner.

Ferdinand now distinguishes colors. Blue — he sneezes or snorts. Yellow — he runs and hides. Red — he makes a short dash and applies all brakes.
Ferdinand counts numbers written on blackboard. Toreador slaps the animal's rump. Ferdinand stamps out count with front paw and stops when kicked by his rear half.
Waltz music: As in Dinkey, all three dance together — and off.

# #63 Football Game

## PROPS:

Shoulder pads, helmets (not necessary)
Dummy stretcher (sides with no bed)
Two balloons

## ACTION:

Two clown teams wearing helmets and shoulder pads run in with much shouting and take their places for the kick-off.
The balloon is held for the kick-off, the referee blows his whistle, and the fullback with a pin in the toe of his shoe kicks and breaks the balloon. Everyone carries on as though the ball were in play, until no one is left standing.
Whistle blows, the players take their places for scrimmage, and the referee produces another balloon.
Quarterback stands close to center to receive ball and hand off to half-back. Several well-practiced plays are run in slow-motion.
Piling up and unpiling also take place in slow motion.
After one play an injured player is left on the field. Stretcher bearers hurry in, place victim between poles, and walk off and over him. Player gets up and rejoins wrong team. Gets pushed back to place.
A "real fancy" play is saved for the finale. Starts at regular speed, then slows down. Runner reverses field, then reverses himself. His own team now wants to tackle him.

All chase runner with ball toward the exit.
The tackle and pile-up occur at the exit, and the balloon bursts.

# #64 Gridiron Heroes

**PROPS:**
Assorted football uniforms, including helmets, shoulder pads, etc.
Two footballs
A length of heavy elastic cord

**ACTION:**
Players are members of one team assembled for signal practice.

They line up in regular formation after a preliminary ball-passing warm-up. An off-tackle play is run in slow motion.

Next, an end run, in regular time, but the ball carrier runs off the floor. He immediately returns, having exchanged the ball for one to which the rubber cord is attached. The other end of the cord is fastened to the ankle of this clown *(Clown 1)*.

Clown 1 lines up at center. When he snaps the ball to the fullback, he lands on his face, as fullback fades back for a pass.

Teammate picks up center, and he promptly falls flat again.

Kick formation is called. Clown 1 is the kicker. He kicks the ball, which returns, knocking over most of the team.

Team lines up again, Clown 1 at center. The play is an end run, and the player with the ball circles the team until cord is stretched to its limit. Ball is released, and all exit in confusion.

# #65 The Hand Is Quicker than the Eye

**PROPS:**
Two drinking glasses                   Pitcher of water
A coin                                  Two handkerchiefs
Card table

**CHARACTERS:**
Clown magician                          Clown

**ACTION:**
*(Card table is placed in center of floor. Clown magician enters carrying the remaining props. He busies himself pouring a glass of water, waving the handkerchiefs, passing the coin from one hand to the other, but picking it out of his hair with the unsuspected hand. A curious clown draws close.)*

**Clown:**
Are you a magician?

**Magician:**
I sure am. Want to see this glass of water disappear? *(He drinks the water.)* That was only fooling. Now watch this coin. See, I put it in this glass. *(He does so.)* Now, see this glass over here? The trick is for me to get the coin to fly from this glass to the other. Do you follow? *(Clown nods.)* Well, you'd better not; there's not that much room in the glass. Observe, I cover the coin and glass with this handkerchief, the other glass with this second handkerchief. A few magic words, and the coin is in the other glass. But that's only half the trick. Now I must get the coin to return to the first glass. A few magic words and presto *(removing handkerchief)*, there it is.

**Clown:**
You're a fake. If you want to see a real trick I can make that coin disappear right before your eyes and you won't even see it.

*(They argue, then bet. Clown puts coin on table. He pours a glass of water and puts the glass over the coin.)*

**Magician:**
You're going to make the coin disappear from under the glass and you say I won't see it go?

**Clown:**
You said it, and I'm not going to put a handkerchief over it, either.

**Magician:**
*(Drawing nearer)* This, I got to see.

**Clown:**
One, two three.

*(On count **three** he grasps the glass, throwing the contents into the magician's face. As magician wipes his eyes, the second clown pockets bets and walks off.)*

# #66 Hot Dog

**PROPS:**
Tray with shoulder straps
Buns, mustard pot, ketchup bottle, knife

**ACTION:**
Clown enters, wearing tray like a cigarette girl. On the tray are buns, mustard and ketchup bottle.
Clown tries to sell hot dogs. He shouts about the merits and length and

flavor of his hot dogs.

He finds a clown customer.

After pocketing a coin from the customer, the salesman cuts open a bun and conspicuously places one well-iodized finger in the roll as the customer winks at a pretty girl in the audience.

Salesman applies mustard or ketchup as requested by the customer.

Hot dog is handed to the customer, and the finger is withdrawn at the same time.

Customer soon discovers he has no wiener and searches the ground for it, assuming it dropped out.

Both clowns circle floor. They meet again and repeat business. Customer is wise after this experience and determines to even the score.

At the third sale the customer grabs the bun and the salesman's wrist and takes a great big bite of the finger. The salesman hollers in pain.

Note: After each of the first two sales, the salesman should lick the condiments off his finger.

# #67 Hot Foot

## PROPS:

Pocket matches

Small firecracker

Bottle of carbonated water

Chair with draped bottom (for hiding bottle)

## ACTION:

Clown sits down on floor to watch an act in progress. He beckons to a second clown and pantomimes need for a chair.

Second clown brings chair; first clown sits in it and goes to sleep.

Second clown decides to play a trick.

He sneaks up on first clown and inserts a small firecracker in the sole of his shoe. Firecracker is lighted. First clown falls forward out of chair as the other clown laughs.

Both clowns go about their business. Finally, second clown sits in chair and goes to sleep.

First clown plants a dud firecracker for the hot foot. Nothing happens when the firecracker should explode.

First clown sneaks up on his hands and knees to investigate. He has a little trouble getting near enough to the foot to be able to see.

## For the ending:

A. Second clown pulls bottle with sprayer out from below chair and puts out the fire, liberally spraying first clown. Or —

B. Second clown can tie a tin can onto the tail of the first clown and place a lighted firecracker in the can.

# #68 How Loud Can You Shout?

**PROPS:**

A vaulting pole or high-jump standard with electric light on an extension cord fastened to it to represent a hydro pole

Some rope

Stage money

Hot water bottle, bandages, clinical thermometer

Throat spray

**ACTION:**

Two clowns lounge around the electric light pole in center of floor.

A third clown enters *(hot water bottle tied to top of his head, bandages around throat, thermometer in mouth, very red nose.)*

Third clown wanders around pathetically, spraying his throat and anyone else who comes too near.

Clowns at post connive. They signal to third, who comes over.

Lights go out except one on post and a floodlight.

Third clown is asked if he would like to see a trick. He nods assent and is then tied to the post.

He is asked how loud he can shout. "Not very loud," he rasps in a hoarse whisper.

"Let's hear you shout for help," says one of the two clowns.

The sick clown tries, but it is a pretty weak shout.

He is urged and encouraged again and again to shout for help, but his cries become more and more feeble until inaudible.

The first two clowns then shake hands with each other and proceed to rifle the third clown's pockets of stage money.

Two clowns walk off, leaving frustrated third clown. Lights flick off. Loud cry for help is heard. Lights come back on. Floor is empty.

# #69 Hypnotics

**PROPS:**

Large sheet, bench, two poles

**ACTION:**

Ringmaster introduces the greatest hypnotist on earth.

Hypnotist enters. He wears long coat with tails, silk hat, mustache, glasses and false nose. He bows. "Thank you for that fine introduction. I expected more. Now may I have a victim, I mean, a volunteer?" Clown volunteer presents himself.

A few magical passes, and the clown is hypnotized:

A. Clown cannot separate his hands when the fingers are interlocked, even when the knee is used for a lever.

B. Clown feels no pain when pin is forced through his hand *(between fingers).*

C. Clown is made as light as a feather. Hypnotist stoops and holds one arm out straight. This the clown straddles. A clown on the far side grasps the hypnotist's wrist. The hypnotized clown is instructed to place his hands on the hypnotist's shoulders. Clown in straddle position is raised and lowered.

Hypnotist brings clown out of trance and calls for more volunteers.

Other clowns have come in. One volunteers.

Hypnotist again makes hypnotic motions, which the clown imitates.

The hypnotist passes out.

Hypnotist falls stiffly backward but is caught before he hits the floor by a clown who lifts him by the neck so that hypnotist falls in another direction, to be caught by a second clown. Repeat.

One catch is not too successful, so hypnotist sits stiffly on floor. One clown pushes the hypnotist's shoulders to the floor, and his feet go to the vertical position. The other clown presses feet back to the floor, and the trunk comes up. Repeat teeter-totter.

Clowns continue teeter-totter, one sitting on his ankles, the other on his shoulders. By alternately squatting and standing, the clowns appear to be taking a ride.

Hypnotist flattens out rigidly. He is picked up by head and ankles and placed on a bench. No amount of finger-snapping revives him, so he is covered by a large sheet.

Hypnotist rises horizontally, to the amazement of the clowns. *(Poles have been suspended on hooks on sides of bench, and under cover of the sheet are brought into position by the hypnotist, who straddles the bench under the cloth and gradually comes to a stand, leaning well backward.)*

Body begins to move off, but a clown is standing on a corner of the sheet and the hypnotist is "exposed."

## #70 The Hypnotist

**PROPS:**

Stage money                    Hand fan
Onion or garlic or leek

**CHARACTERS:**

Clown hypnotist                Clown subject

**ACTION:**

*(Clown hypnotist comes to center of floor. Announcement, acknowledgment, etc. Hypnotist asks for assistant or volunteer. Another clown is quick to offer his services. Hypnotist makes it clear that when subject is hypnotized*

*he will not be able to get up alone.)*

**Subject:**
You mean to say that if I am put on the floor I won't be able to get up alone?

**Hypnotist:**
That's right. You can't get up alone.

*(Bets are made with stage money. Hypnotist makes his fancy passes, but the subject does not succumb.)*

**Hypnotist:**
This is more difficult than I thought. However, my blitz method never fails.

*(He signals for assistant to bring in the fan and onion. Hypnotist holds onion in front of subject and waves fan back and forth until subject is overcome. Hypnotist lies down beside him.)*

**Subject:**
*(Looking at hypnotist)* Which one of us is hypnotized?

**Hypnotist:**
You are. Now let's see you get up alone.

*(Subject and hypnotist get up at the same time. Hypnotist pockets bets and walks off.)*

# #71 Ice for Mrs. Smaltz

**PROPS:**

| | |
|---|---|
| Iceman's uniform | Ice in varying sizes |
| Ice tongs | Sugar tongs |
| Sponge | |

**ACTION:**
Clown is dressed as iceman. Word "ICE" appears on apron and on hat.
Clown enters carrying large block of ice by tongs or in waterproof bag.
Clown circles the floor and exits. En route he calls, "Fifty pounds of ice for Mrs. Smaltz. Is Mrs. Smaltz here?"
Since Mrs. Smaltz does not claim her ice, the clown returns at the next opportunity. The same performance is repeated, but the ice is about half the former size.
This goes on until the ice has diminished in size so that a refrigerator ice cube is carried by a pair of sugar tongs. By this time the iceman is getting desperate and he asks several ladies, "Are you positive you are not Mrs. Smaltz?"
For his final round the clown carries a wet sponge which he squeezes each time he makes the call, "Fifty pounds of ice for Mrs. Smaltz."

# #72 Information, Please

**PROPS:**

Real piano
Five chairs
Five dummy microphones

Two tables, draped
Five toy machine guns, or flash guns

**CHARACTERS:**

The M.C. (ringmaster)
A pianist

Four quiz experts (clowns)

**SCENE:**

TV Quiz Program. M.C. has small table on one side; the experts sit at a longer
table on opposite side. Everyone has a "mike." Pianist and piano are
suitably placed.

**ACTION:**

The M.C. announces that all the questions this evening are on music.

The experts are asked to identify the title of the selections and the composers.
"Do the experts understand? Then here is our first selection."

The laugh is that the pianist always plays the same arrangements of chords
for all selections as called for by the M.C.

The clowns guess: Wagner, Brahms, Sousa, etc. Also, they call out names
of well-known arias and operas: *Barber of Seville, Carmen* etc. *(There
should be no hesitation in calls.)*

Of course, they are never right.

M.C. becomes more and more desperate as he continues to hand out
mythical money to people who are alleged to have sent in the titles.

At last, the M.C. goes to the pianist and whispers in his ear.

Returning to place, he takes out a toy machine gun from under his table
and announces that the experts will have one more chance.

The pianist plays a few bars of the most popular current hit, one that everyone knows *(or a well-known "oldie")*.

Experts are stumped. They go into a huddle. They start to answer, then
check themselves.

They are mortally shot by the M.C. Experts slouch in place with heads
buried on the table. This gives them a chance to reach for their guns
which are under table.

A "plant" in the audience asks the M.C. to identify the tune. He asks
the pianist to replay it.

The M.C. is stumped. He gets red in the face. Asks if the audience has
any other requests. They call on him to name the tune.

Experts simultaneously come to life and shoot the M.C. All die. *(Lights
out)*

# #73 In the Days of the Model T

**PROPS:**
Materials to build a make-believe auto: packing boxes, flashlights for head-
lamps, etc.
A tin can containing some pebbles
A firecracker in large tin can
A number of inflated balloons
Five car rugs

**CHARACTERS:**
Henry, the driver, in old-fashioned costume
Lizzie, the back-seat driver (also costumed)
Five clowns (The clowns are the four wheels and the spare. They are covered
with car rugs under which they hide two balloons each.)

**SCENE:**
Lights go out, and car is assembled in middle of floor. The firecracker is
placed in the tin can, and the tin can is positioned where the motor
would be, with fuse facing the driver.
Characters take their places.

**ACTION:**
Car starts by cranking. Lizzie shakes tin with pebbles. Henry gets in. Car
stops. Repeat.
Henry drives. Much sticking out of hands.
Lizzie says she'll tell him when it's going to rain.
Much back-seat driving.
One tire goes flat. *(Balloon deflated by pin.)*
Henry jacks up car and replaces tire by carrying in spare.
Other tires go flat one at a time. *(Clowns slide out flat on stomachs. As
the tire is pumped up they return to hands-and-knees position.)*
Henry tests each tire after inflating by kicking it.
On signal the four tires go flat simultaneously.
Henry nonchalantly lights a cigarette and in the process sets alight the fuse
to the firecracker.
Firecracker goes off.
Henry and Lizzie fall off seats. Lights go off.

# #74 Just Before Intermission

**PROPS:**
Four plastic golf bags with clubs          Four plastic golf balls

Three indoor putting cups

**CHARACTERS:**

Four clown golfers                              One clown messenger

**SCENE:**

This is the last act before intermission.

Four clown golfers saunter onto the floor carrying golf equipment. As they warm up, stagehands try to make the gym look like a golf course.

If this act follows a gymnastic number the apparatus and mats serve as traps and hazards.

The putting cups are placed in three corners of the gym.

**ACTION:**

The golfers tee off from the corner where there is no putting cup.

All play in order toward first hole.

The golfers exaggerate everything they do. Argue count. Show extreme anguish or glee, alibi, and the like.

Trick clubs, clubs that have extra flexible shafts or that break in two, may be used.

When they are holing out on the first hole a clown messenger wheels or runs in and delivers a telegram to Clown 1. Clown 1 opens envelope and reads: "Your house is being consumed by fire. Rush home!"

The telegram is thrown aside, and the game continues as though nothing had happened.

As they come to the second hole the messenger rushes in with a telegram for Clown 2. Clown 2 reads: "Your wife has been taken to the hospital. Serious." Again the game continues unconcernedly.

Approaching the third hole, the messenger has a telegram for Clown 3. Clown 3 reads the telegram, drops it and runs in all haste toward the exit.

All clowns look puzzled. Clown 4 picks up the telegram, reads it and disappears in a hurry.

Clown 1 picks up the telegram, and Clown 2 says, "Read it out loud."

Clown 1 reads: "Refreshments now being served. Get a nice cold drink and a hot dog. Two thin dimes will get you the works. No extra charge for mustard."

Clowns 1 and 2 start to rush off, bump into each other, fall down, get tied up, and finally almost make the exit as Clowns 3 and 4 lead the refreshment caterers onto the floor.

# #75 A Kissing Game

A wrestling mat is centered on the floor in the middle of which stand three or four clowns.

For each of these clowns there is an inflated lace-up ball to which a 30-foot length of cord is attached. These balls are placed about halfway between the clowns and the outside edge of the mat.

The free end of each cord is held by some girl in the audience. **(Girl** can *be interpreted loosely to include any female from 8 to 80.)*

Another clown sits down on the floor so as not to interfere *(too much)* with the action. He has a pair of dice.

The ringmaster explains the game as follows.

The clown will roll the dice and then shout out the total of the spots that are uppermost — somewhere from 2 to 12. If the total is 7 or 11 the ladies must yank the cords so as to get the ball off the mat before a clown pounces on it. If a lady jerks her ball free of the mat, she will receive a bag of candy kisses. *But* — should she fail, she must kiss the clown on the cheek, and if she fails to keep her part of the bargain, then the clown will kiss her on the cheek. There is also a penalty for anyone jerking the ball off the mat should the total not be 7 or 11, and that is elimination. There is, too, a bonus. Should a clown tackle a ball when the score is other than 7 or 11, then that ball will be advanced one yard nearer the edge of the mat.

Play about five minutes. Have one practice call.

The clowns should try to excite the competitors. For example, the clown rolling the dice can move his lips as though counting up to 7 or 11 and then shout any other number. Likewise, the other clowns can pretend they are going to leap on a ball.

If a ball is jerked off on a wrong number, the competitor is eliminated and should receive a candy sucker. The ringmaster or another clown can make the award and pass on the cord quickly to someone else.

When a bag of kisses is won, the cord should be handed to someone else nearby.

Remember that the audience is more apt to enjoy the actions and reactions of some of the older "girls."

# #76 Little Sir Echo

**PROPS:**
Spotlight
Screen
Piano
Public-address system with two microphones

**SETTING:**
Announcements indicate that a well-known singer will entertain with a solo.

Soloist and piano accompanist enter and take their places.

Soloist is under the spotlight where microphone has been placed.

A second singer is hidden behind screen, where he has microphone 2.

**ACTION:**
The first singer announces that his first song is an old one. *("Little Sir Echo" is a suggestion because it permits repeats or echo lines.)*

Song is presented in straightforward manner toward audience, but amazement is shown when unseen singer echoes from behind curtain. Singer is not too pleased with acoustics; stops, repeats, same result. Singer moves to new location followed by spotlight. Procedures are repeated.

Singer apologizes to audience for the poor acoustics, explaining that he wouldn't mind so much if the echo were in tune.

The echo answers, "What's the matter with my voice? It's as good as yours, you fugitive from a canary cage!" Singer digs out the echo, and the two sing a duet.

# #77 Magic Pills

**PROPS:**
A small stand covered with cloth
Some imitation pills (mints)
A telescope

**CHARACTERS:**
Clown barker                    Hick clown

**ACTION:**
*(Clown barker sets up his stand and announces his "Marvelous Travel Pills.")*

**Barker:**
Just make up your mind where you want to go, take a pill, and presto, there you are.

*(Hick clown comes in. He listens to the spiel and says he would like to take a sea trip. Barker says that will be a white pill. He gives Hick a white one.)*

**Barker:**
Just a minute, I'll go with you. *(He takes one, too. Both begin to look queer and unsteady.)* Hurrah! We're off.

**Hick:**
Yes, away off. *(Hick takes telescope from his pocket and focuses on the audience.)* My goodness. We're sure at sea. Look at all the fish.

**Barker:**
*(Takes telescope.)* Look at that wave!

**Hick:**
I'll bet it's a Toni.

**Barker:**
*(As clown goes by eating hot dog)* What a roll.

**Hick:**
*(Rolling considerably)* Among your travel pills have you got a seasick pill?

**Barker:**
Who cares about a seasick pill? It's me who's getting seasick. Where's the bucket? *(He hands glass back to Hick.)*

**Hick:**
*(Looking through glass)* Hold everything.

**Barker:**
*(Holding his stomach)* That's what I'm doing.

**Hick:**
The sun's coming up. I see it over there. *(Points at audience.)*

**Barker:**
*(Looking through glass)* Sun nothing, you dope. That's a bald head. *(Blackout)*

# #78 The Manly Art
## (Comedy Boxing)

**PROPS:**
Boxing gloves and other regular equipment
Gong, screen, clown mallet, seltzer bottles, sponges, pails of water

**CHARACTERS:**

| | |
|---|---|
| One well-known boxer | Referee |
| Announcer | Timekeeper |
| Seconds | Clowns, as noted |

**ACTION:**
The bout is announced between well-known local boy and the challenger to the world's professional title *(kind permission of AAU)*.

Boxer takes place in ring. Nothing else happens. Whispered conversation with announcer, who tells audience that the other boxer's car has broken down, and won't someone please volunteer to take his place. Clown volunteers.

***Round 1:***
Both come out of corners fast, but clown trips and rolls under or by boxer. Clown gets up shadow boxing and snorting in wrong direction. They clinch. Clown punches himself by mistake. Boxer gets clown in head-lock and gives him a couple of terrific uppercuts. A third wallop causes the clown to reel around the ring. The bell rings, and clown sits on boxer's lap in wrong corner.

**Round 2:**

The clown is being badly beaten. They clinch. In the clinch the clown takes off boxer's belt. Each time the boxer pauses to pull up his trunks *(shorts underneath)*, the clown gets in a punch.

**Round 3:**

The clown maneuvers the boxer so that the boxer has his back to the screen behind which the clown has a clown accomplice with a big mallet. The boxer is unaware of this and once or twice just when he is due to get the hammer he steps out of place. *(Accomplice is on a stepladder.)*

Accomplice knocks out boxer. Referee holds up clown's hand. Accomplice tries to hit referee but falls off ladder, and there is a general pile-up in the middle of the ring.

This should be well-rehearsed.

There should be added comedy between rounds as the seconds go to work with seltzer bottles, sponges. The timekeeper may announce, "When you hear the next musical note, there will be exactly 289 shopping days before Christmas."

# #79 Mary Had a Little Lamb

**PROPS:**

A screen, a stool
A watering can
An umbrella (large bulb syringe attached to handle and rubber tube leading along shaft through top of umbrella)

**CHARACTERS:**

Four clowns

**ACTION:**

Screen is placed in desired location. Stool behind screen.

Clown A and his clown stooge enter. Clown A carries watering can filled with water.

These two hold a whispered consultation. The stooge goes behind screen, taking watering can with him, and stands on stool so he can look over top of screen.

Clown B enters, and Clown A maneuvers B in front of screen and stooge.

Clown A asks B if he can recite. Clown B acts dumb, so A says the following two lines and then has B repeat them:

> "Mary had a little lamb, its fleece was white as snow,
> And everywhere that Mary went, the lamb was sure to go."

When B is successful A asks him if he would like to try the second verse. A then recites the second verse with a knowing wink at the stooge.

"Mary went for a walk one day, down a shady lane,
And all of a sudden, all of a sudden — down came the rain."

Stooge indicates he knows what to do by showing the watering can which
  B does not see.
B now tries the rhyme three times, but each time, he muffs the cue and
  instead of the proper four words he substitutes:

- she went insane
- she felt a sharp pain
- along came a train

With each repeat, A corrects B, saying, "No, no, *down came the rain.*"
A gets more and more annoyed and pushes B slightly each time so that A
  is eventually immediately below the stooge. The last *down came the
  rain* is shouted by A, who receives the contents of the watering can.
B holds out his hand, noting the downpour, and exits, leaving A.
C now enters carrying folded umbrella. He is much quicker than B, and as
  A tries the stunt again he is sure he has a real victim.
C gets the second verse right the first time, but raises his umbrella in time
  to miss the rainfall.
C points his umbrella at A, squeezes the syringe which is filled with water,
  and A gets his second bath.
C exits, holding the umbrella over his head. Water spurts in intervals from
  the umbrella. A follows disconsolately.

# #80 Masquerade

## PROPS:
One garbage can                          Sign: TWO GARBAGE CANS

## ACTION:
A clown enters and paces up and down. Clown is obviously very worried.
Second clown comes in and asks first clown, "What's wrong?"
First clown says he has to go to a masquerade and doesn't know what
  to wear.
Second clown makes suggestions and strikes pose in imitation of each:
  Napoleon, King Tut, Marilyn Monroe, Charlie Chaplin, Superman.
First clown finds none of the above satisfactory, shaking his head at each
  suggestion.
Second clown exclaims, "I've got it!" He whistles, and a third clown brings
  in a garbage can.
First clown is made to hold the can under one arm. He naturally wants
  to know what it is all about, but the other two "shush" him.
Second clown whistles again, and a fourth clown brings in a sign which is
  hung on first clown's back.
First clown wants to know what the sign says, but second clown says, "Never

mind. If the masquerade is a good one the audience will applaud."

First clown is led around the gym so that the audience can read the sign —
TWO GARBAGE CANS.

Clowns three and four get the audience to applaud.

At the exit, the first clown takes a bow. Others give him the raspberry.
First clown can reach in the garbage can to extract a banana or other
desirable item. He exits eating food.

# #81 Mathematics

## PROPS
Blackboard                                Chalk
Bench                                     Dunce cap

## CHARACTERS:
One miner with blackened face and hands
Three clowns

## ACTION:
*(Blackboard is placed at one end of room, bench in front. Hat under bench.
Clowns sit on bench and doodle on board. Puzzled miner comes in studying
paycheck. He shows it to clowns.)*

## First Clown:
You say you get $13 a day? *(Miner nods.)* And you work seven days a
week? *(Miner nods.)* And your paycheck for the week is $28? *(Miner
nods. Clowns try to work it out on fingers.)*

## First Clown:
Something's wrong here. Let's try division. *(He goes to the board and
works out the division, explaining the figures as he goes.)*

|                          |                                                        |
|--------------------------|--------------------------------------------------------|
| 7)28 ( 13                | $28 a week. Write down 28.                             |
|   7            | 7 days a week. Write down 7.                           |
|  21                 | 7 into 2 won't go. 7 into 8 goes once.                 |
|                          |   Write 1.                                    |
|  21                 | Write 7 below 28.                                       |

7 from 28 leaves 21. Write 21.
   7 into 21 goes 3 times. Write 3.
3 times 7 = 21. Write 21 below.

That comes out even, so you must be getting $13 a day. *(Circle 13.
Second clown shows disgust. Putting dunce cap on first clown, he
goes to the board.)*

## Second Clown:
Division is no way to solve a difficult problem like this. You must use multi-
plication.

| | |
|---|---|
| 13 | $13 a day. Write down 13. |
| 7 | 7 days a week. Write down 7. |
| 21 | 7 times 3 is 21. Write down 21. |
| 7 | Only one figure left to multiply: 7 |
| | times 1 makes 7. Write down 7. |
| 28 | 21 and 7 makes 28. Write down 28. And |
| | that comes out even. |

What does you paycheck say? Yep, that's right. Twenty-eight dollars.

*(Third clown puts dunce cap on second clown.)*

**Third Clown:**
You're both wrong. This problem is one of addition. Let me show you.

| | |
|---|---|
| 13 | Monday = $13. Write 13. |
| 13 | Tuesday = etc. |
| 13 | |
| 13 | |
| 13 | |
| 13 | |
| 13 | Now we add the threes. 3, 6, etc., 21. Write it. |
| 21 | Now the ones. 1, 2, etc., 7. Write it. |
| 7 | 21 and 7. That's 28. Write it. |
| 28 | |

*(All look puzzled.)*

**Third Clown:**
Mr. Miner, you're a very lucky man to make $13 a day.

*(All congratulate miner and walk off.)*

# #82 Mental Telepathy

**PROPS:**
One blackboard, chalk, eraser
Stand to hold blackboard
Two hats (beanies) with antenna on each
One blindfold

**CHARACTERS:**
Three clowns (one can be a farmer; ringmaster may substitute for Clown 1)

**ACTION:**
Clowns 1 and 2 set up equipment.
Farmer enters.
Clowns 1 and 2 separate and mimic action of transmitting thought waves.
Farmer wants to know what it is all about.

Clown 1 offers to give demonstration.

Blindfold is placed on Clown 2, and farmer is asked to write down any number on the blackboard.

Clown 1 asks Clown 2 for the number, slapping him on the back the required number of times.

Farmer smartens up finally and indicates he has discovered a number to stump the other two. He writes down 0 for zero.

Clown 1 looks baffled, but solves the problem by kicking Clown 2, who yells, "Oh!"

## #83 Mexican Jumping Beans

*(A well-known gymnasium game)*

**PROPS:**
Straw hats for all the clowns
Long sash cord weighted at one end with bean bag filled with shot

**MUSIC:**
"Mexican Hat Dance"

**ACTIONS:**
Clowns wearing large, floppy straw hats rush in to the accompaniment of music.

One clown carries the weighted sash cord and he sits or lies on the floor with the others forming a circle about him.

The center clown whirls the weight around his head, gradually easing out the rope with the weight traveling about a foot off the floor. When the weight reaches the other clowns they are forced to jump rope.

From a slow start the rope is speeded up until traveling rapidly. Fun is created by the action of the clowns in leaping the rope and in getting caught.

Each time a clown is caught the game is restarted.

One clown reverses matters by flopping flat on the floor so the rope passes over him. He raises and lowers his head as the rope circles.

Finally, one clown forgets to jump, and the rope encircles his ankles several times like a lasso. Other clowns drag him off like a trussed pig.

## #84 Midway Barkers

**PROPS:**
Three megaphones                    Bunch of celery
Three soapboxes

**CHARACTERS:**
Three clowns

**ACTION:**
Clowns run out with megaphones and stand on boxes — one box per
   clown — and the three in line.
Ringmaster informs audience that they are at the midway, "and before
   us we have three of the most sensational exhibits — no, not the barkers
   which you see on the boxes — but what you don't see beyond the
   painted canvases.
"These three midway barkers will tell you about their extraordinary attrac-
   tions. And we want you good people to tell us who is the best barker.
"First, we have Houdini, the man of a thousand escapes.
"Second, there is Emma, the fattest woman in the world.
"Third, you will hear about 'Stretcho,' the India rubber man."
On the word *go*, the three barkers broadcast simultaneously for 30 seconds,
   when the ringmaster eventually stops them.
Each barker should have a carefully rehearsed script which lends itself to
   numerous gestures and antics.
They should pay absolutely no attention to the others, giving an all-out
   performance for their part of the midway crowd.
The ringmaster declares the contest a draw, and in order to determine a
   winner, each will enact how he would perform if he found a hair in a
   bowl of soup at the Greasy Spoon Restaurant.
The audience claps for the winner, who is presented with a bunch of celery.

# #85 Musical Treat

**PROPS:**

| | |
|---|---|
| Cap pistol | Toy cannon |
| Swimming pool rescue hook | Toy rubber frog |

**CHARACTERS:**
Miss How-She-Can-Holler, a mess of a soprano
Professor Ivory, at the piano
(The singer, a man dressed as a lady, is very la-de-da. The professor
wears a wig and large horn-rimmed glasses.)

**ACTION:**
The master of ceremonies makes the introduction, saying what a privilege
   it is to have such outstanding talent on the program and that it is
   hoped they will receive the full attention of the audience.
The song to be sung by Miss How-She-Can-Holler is — *(the M.C. goes
   to the piano to look at the sheet music and reads)* "Refrain from
   Spitting."
Professor enters, followed by the artist. Professor sits at piano and sounds
   key of C. Singer "mi-mi's." Her voice is very husky, and the professor

looks in her throat, extracting the frog which he had concealed in his hand.

Terrific introduction by the professor — either in pantomime or dubbed in from P.A. system.

The singer starts to sing in high falsetto and carries on in spite of frantic gestures by the professor, who stops playing and tries to stop her.

In desperation he takes out cap pistol and fires it. Miss How-She-Can-Holler is too engrossed to notice the bullet except that she spits out a piece of lead onto the floor.

She still sings.

Professor gets out cannon.

In meantime, she coughs slightly and, in covering her mouth with a hanky, slips in a small rubber ball. Cannon is fired. She spits out ball. She still sings.

Professor and others come in with big hook and drag her off the floor.

Note: Instead of singing, Miss How-She-Can-Holler could make mouth motions and gestures to synchronize with violent recorded music.

# #86 Niagara Falls

## PROPS:

Drinking glass

Large funnel

Jug of water

Hot water bottle

## ACTION:

Two clowns enter with their equipment — water jug, glass and funnel. They obviously are up to something.

A rube clown enters and becomes the victim.

He is asked if he has ever been to Niagara Falls. The clown says *no* and is then informed that they will teach him a stunt that everyone in Niagara Falls knows.

"The object of this stunt is to drop a coin from one's forehead into a funnel held in the trouser belt," the clowns explain. They proceed to place a funnel in the rube's trousers in the waist front and they tilt his head back, placing a coin on his forehead.

On the count of three the clown is to raise his head and drop the coin into the funnel. Whether successful or not, the "goat" is asked to repeat the stunt a second and a third time.

The third time, one of the two clowns pours part of a glassful of water down the funnel as the other makes sure the head is held in the right position.

The "goat" jumps around shaking one foot vigorously while the other two give him the laugh.

A moment later a fourth clown enters, and the former victim asks him the question, "Have you ever been to Niagara Falls?" The other two clowns stay to assist, and the gag is repeated.

However, when the water is poured down the funnel, the new "goat"

97

gives no sign that anything is wrong.

Clown keeps holding victim's head back and delaying the stunt while the others pour more and more water down the funnel. Clowns look up the "goat's" pant leg and act puzzled.

When the water jug is empty, the "goat" takes a hot water bottle out of his trousers *(into which he had inserted the funnel)* and, waving it in the air, he runs off.

# #87 Palmist

## PROPS:
A round table, draped in cloth
Two chairs
Appropriate signs
A crystal gazing ball or good facsimile
Paintbrush
Tin of red paint or solution to look like paint

## SCENE:
The table with crystal ball in center is placed in position.

Signs are located. Chairs on opposite sides of table. The palmist, wearing a turban and a long flowing robe, sits on chair before the table. He gazes intently into the crystal ball, the scene illuminated by one spotlight.

Paintbrush and paint are under the table, hidden by the cloth.

## ACTION:
*(Clown enters and cirles about in shadows, gradually getting closer and closer until he stands before the palmist. Palmist finally looks up and waves customer into the other seat.)*

**Palmist:**
*(In deep Oriental voice)* And what do you want?

**Customer:**
I want my palm read.

**Palmist:**
Would you please say that again so that there is no mistake?

**Customer:**
I want my palm read.

**Palmist:**
Very well, it shall be well-read.

*(He takes customer's right hand and places it on the table palm up. He scrutinizes palm for a moment, then asks customer to close his eyes. Palmist then smears the palm with the red paint. Customer is awfully mad and threatens to punch cowering mystic in the nose.)*

**Palmist:**
Remember, you said you wanted it red.

*(Customer looks at his hand and starts to laugh at the joke on himself. He pats palmist on the back with his clean left hand.)*

**Customer:**
OK. Good joke. No hard feelings. Shake hands.

*(Palmist stands up, and they shake hands — right hands. Both show surprise, then laugh at the two red hands and they walk off together.)*

# #88 Photography I

## PROPS:
A five-gallon rectangular tin (maple syrup) to represent the body of a camera, and a small round tin soldered on the end serving as a lens. The open end of the small tin faces outward, and a hole is cut so as to connect the two tins.
All the above mounted on a tripod
Photographer's black cloth
Two large syringes (or squirt guns), one bucket of water and a cap pistol
One birdie such as the "whirligigs" sold on midways

## ACTION:
Clown photographer enters and sets up his camera, complaining that this is no time or place for a professional photographer to take portraits.
Second clown gets curious and is persuaded to pose.
The birdie has been placed inside the lens, and during the arranging of the subject the photographer hands him the black thread attached to the bird.
Photographer gets set. Subject mugs.
"Now watch the birdie."
Cap pistol is fired by photographer from under cloth. Bird flies out and is waved excitedly by subject.
Photographer indicates that a second take is necessary. Procedure is repeated except that subject is placed very close to the camera.
This time the photographer squirts a stream of water through the lens into the subject's face.
Camera man runs to the other end of the gym and again sets up his equipment.
Second clown subject is secured.
While the photographer is under his cloth the first clown subject ostentatiously fills a syringe from the water bucket.
Photographer, from under cloth: "Watch the birdie."
First subject, in stage whisper, as he places syringe in lens opening: "I'll bet this birdie can swim."

He lets photographer have it. All run off.
Note: Instead of cap pistol, camera could be equipped with regular camera
flash.

## #89 Photography II

**PROPS:**
Fake camera, with flash or cap pistol attached
Collapsible stand
Baby buggy, rattle, baby's bottle

**CHARACTERS:**

Baby (smallest tumbler)          Clown photographer
Clown mother and father

**ACTION:**
Photographer enters and attempts to drum up business.
Couple enters, pushing baby carriage containing baby. Baby is using
    bottle.
All meet.
Photographer makes up to baby, using rattle.
Parents agree to a photograph.
Photographer poses parents and baby in a number of ridiculous positions.
When set for the picture, photographer points father's face in one direc-
    tion, the wife's in another. Photographer kisses wife. Baby tries to
    attract father's attention.
Picture is "fired." Camera collapses.
In the confusion the baby gets out of carriage and hikes for exit. Parents
    scream and chase, and baby exits, turning cartwheels or handsprings.

## #90 Photography III

**PROPS:**
Clown camera with flash or gun
Some pictures of Hollywood picture stars
Sign: PICTURES DEVELOPED WHILE YOU WAIT

**ACTION:**
Clown photographer solicits business from the audience. He probably
    will not be successful, so clowns volunteer.
Business of posing subject.
Photographer says, "I suppose you would like to see the birdie." Subject
    nods head. "Well, we'll have you look at a real live bird." He points
    out girl in the audience.
Subject stares at "bird" until he is presented with his photo.

Photographer goes about the business of taking the picture, remarking on the close resemblance of the subject to one of the photographs he has in his collection.

Picture is taken. Subject stares. Photographer leaves the room and returns after the next act.

He brings the subject out of his trance and gives him his photo.

Subject is so pleased he wades through the audience to show the picture to his "birdie."

# #91 Play Ball

## PROPS:
Slapstick for bat
Ball
Catcher's mit
Hand mirror
A specially prepared shirt, with at least six yards of material sewed on the tail as an extension
Bird cage from which bottom is missing
Balloon and tube

## ACTION:
Clowns run on and take their places for a game.

Pantomime action.

Batter comes up with slapstick.

Catcher dons bird cage for mask.

After each pitch, catcher goes up to talk to pitcher. Pitcher can't hear until he opens door of cage.

Umpire goes forward, crossing plate, to speed up catcher-pitcher business. Batter accidentally takes practice swing at right moment to hit umpire on the seat.

Umpire falls flat, unconscious. A swelling begins to develop where he was hit. *(This is balloon and tube.)* It swells until exploded.

Game resumes. New batter.

This batter has a hand mirror which he holds out in front to catch the catcher's signals.

Umpire can't see mirror, but catcher does. Catcher argues with umpire, and batter slips mirror inside shirt.

This is repeated. Argument gets hot.

Catcher points where he thinks mirror is hidden. Some feeling around and undoing of shirt buttons on batter.

Umpire and catcher now begin to pull off batter's trick shirt over his head. This, of course, has no end and should be fed out slowly.

Other players have come in and hold on to batter so that it becomes a tug of war as catcher and umpire back up toward exit.

Shirt finally comes off, and all fall over backward.

Batter can have words tattooed on his chest or back: "Love Those Bums."

# #92 Poor Fido

**PROPS:**
Some sickbed utensils
Radio on table, with a speaker hooked up to an offstage microphone

**ACTION:**
Radio is set at one side of the gym.
Clowns come in, turn radio on, and sit down on floor to listen to program.
Voice is heard, along with appropriate static:
"Station B-U-N-K and the time is exactly ___ .
  Miss Lott Noise will now sing, 'Take Back Your Heart; I Ordered Liver and Onions.' *(Clowns hold hands over their ears. Loud static.)* Thank you, Miss Lotta Noise. As usual this program is brought to you by the _____ Laundry whose motto is, 'Don't tear your clothes to pieces on the washboard; let our machines do it for you.' *(Clowns rock with laughter.)*
"And now for our feature story. *(Clowns get really attentive and draw closer to radio.)* This is a story of Poor Fido.
"Mr. Brown owned a little dog named Fido. *(Clowns pet imaginary dog.)* Now Fido was very bad about following Mr. Brown when he went to the office in the morning. *(Shake heads disapprovingly.)* One morning Mr. Brown threw a rock at Fido to scare him back home and accidentally killed Poor Fido dead. *(Clowns blow noses, etc.)*
"Mr. Brown didn't know what to do with Fido's body, but he had a neighbor he didn't like, so he skinned Poor Fido *(clowns shudder)* and gave him to the neighbor as a rabbit. The neighbor thought this very kind of Mr. Brown and thanked him pro- . . . pro- . . . a lot. *(Clowns nudge each other knowingly.)*
"However, the neighbor was immediately called out of town on business, so he gave Poor Fido *(the rabbit)* to Aunt Jemima, who did the laundry for everyone on the block.
"That night when Mr. Brown was returning home from the office, he passed Aunt Jemima's house. She waved at him *(clowns ditto)* and said, 'Yoo-hoo, Mr. Brown, won't you come in and have supper with me? I've got a fine mess of rabbit stew.' *(Clowns begin to anticipate.)*
"Now, Mr. Brown knew that Aunt Jemima had a fine reputation as a cook and, since his wife was away, decided this would be an excellent opportunity to sample Auntie's cooking. *(Clowns rub stomachs.)* After he had gorged himself on rabbit stew until he could hold no more, Mr. Brown asked Aunt Jemima, 'How did you ever come to find such a nice fat rabbit?'
" 'Why, bless your heart,' she chuckled. 'Your neighbor was going out of town today, so he gave me this nice fact rabbit this morning.' *(Clowns*

*are convulsed.)*

"Mr. Brown rose weakly from his chair *(clowns ditto)*, staggered to the kitchen door *(clowns ditto)*, leaned helplessly against the house *(clowns ditto)*, and said, 'Fido, I have called you many times, but this is one time you are going to come without calling.' *(Clowns take sick room utensils out of their costumes and stagger off floor.)*

"Good night, everybody. Pleasant dreams."

# #93 Racing Ducks

## PROPS:
A large pan or rubber receptacle for holding water, to represent a pond
Two celluloid or plastic ducks
Stage money
Two blindfolds
Oxygen tank
Bicycle pump
A pie tin filled with flour

## ACTION:
The pond is placed in the center of the floor.

Two clowns approach the pond and become interested. In turn they produce their bathtub ducks. Lots of fun sailing ducks.

They blow on the ducks and soon conceive the idea of a race.

A race is staged, and after one or two false starts, one duck obviously wins.

The winner gets obnoxiously conceited and boasts that his duck is the best racer in the world. The other challenges him to a second race.

Betting is heavy.

Race is rerun.

The loser does a bit of thinking as the other pockets the wager and then says, "You may have the faster duck, but I've got more wind."

More betting.

To settle this bet one duck is placed in the center of the pond, and clowns take opposite sides and pantomime that the object is to blow the duck toward the opponent's side.

One or two practice blows are permitted.

One clown then claims he can beat the other blindfolded for a million bucks. Bets are placed.

One clown goes to the oxygen tank. A third clown carries in a bicycle pump and proceeds to inflate the other contestant.

Clowns take their places. Duck is positioned. Clowns are blindfolded. Third clown has prepared himself as starter.

Two more clowns sneak in and replace the pond with a pan of flour.

Results are obvious.

# #94 The Raw Recruit

**PROPS:**
A number of dummy guns with which to fire caps, or rifles with blanks
Volleyball painted black with long rubber cord attached (bomb)
Postcard or photo
Notepad or pencil
Sergeant's uniform

**CHARACTERS:**
A tough sergeant
Several clowns who serve as raw recruits
The misfit — "Hopeless"

**ACTION:**
*(Sergeant leads men in brief drill.)*

**Sergeant:**
We will now take the roll.

*(Takes out pad and pencil. Hopeless does forward roll on floor, then backs sheepishly into line.)*

**Sergeant:**
What's your name?

**Hopeless:**
Hopeless.

**Sergeant:**
I should think so. *(Writing)* And the initials?

**Hopeless:**
I.M.H.

**Sergeant:**
*(Writing and repeating aloud)* I am hopeless.

**Hopeless:**
I think so, too.

**Sergeant:**
Married or single?

**Hopeless:**
Why?

**Sergeant:**
It's only a matter of form. *(Hopeless whistles.)* Smoke?

**Hopeless:**
Don't mind if I do. *(Sergeant knocks him down.)*

**Sergeant:**
All ready for target practice! *(Men lie down with guns at ready.)* Now I want to see you hit the bull's-eye. *(Sergeant stands forward and to one side. His back to the line of fire, he shields eyes and bends forward. Guns go off. Sergeant jumps, grabbing pants.)* Who did that? *(All jump to feet, saluting.)* I said, "Hit the bull's-eye."

**Hopeless:**
Please, sir, the bull was looking the other way.

**Sergeant:**
Come here. I've a good mind to have you shot at sunrise.

**Hopeless:**
But I don't get up that early.

**Sergeant:**
In that case take your gun and go off and shoot yourself and save us the trouble.

*(Hopeless salutes and retires. Sergeant drills rest of men. A shot is heard offstage.)*

**Sergeant:**
Great Scott! He's killed himself.

**Hopeless:**
*(Staggering back in and weeping)* I missed again. *(He weeps on Sergeant's shoulder.)*

**Sergeant:**
Here, here. You'll have better luck next time.

**Hopeless:**
Yes, but I just got a letter from my wife and she sent me a picture of our little boy — our little boy that I've never seen. Isn't he cute? *(Showing picture)* Doesn't he look like Cupid?

**Sergeant:**
That's a funny-looking boy. He has no hair on his head. *(Hopeless says nothing, but looks at picture over sergeant's shoulder, then turns the card bottom-side-up.)* Here, take this bomb to the arsenal and don't drop it.

*(He gives Hopeless the bomb. One of the soldiers manages to get hold of the end of the elastic cord. Hopeless retires carrying the bomb. The Sergeant turns to face men and straddles the cord with back to Hopeless. A gun is fired. The bomb is released. Sergeant is knocked down. Mutiny, etc.)*

# #95 The Realtor

**PROPS:**

| | |
|---|---|
| Signs as indicated | Baby carriage, baby bottle |

Gun                                    Silk hat
Stage money

**CHARACTERS:**
Clown realtor                          Clown farmer
Clown wife                             Clown baby

**ACTION:**
Pompous clown wearing silk hat enters and sets up a number of real estate
  signs: FOR RENT, FOR SALE, WILL SUBDIVIDE, LOT WITH A
  VIEW, etc.
Clown realtor rubs his hands and prepares for business.
Farmer and his wife come in. Wife is pushing a baby carriage which contains
  clown baby with bottle.
Family looks over signs, with agent following at discreet distance. When
  the family stops to admire "lot with a view," the realtor goes to work
  on his sales talk. He is quiet but enthusiastic. His final recommendation
  is the echo for which the place is famous. He demonstrates, shouting,
  "Yoo-hoo!"
The echo is returned by an accomplice offstage, or the public-address
  system may be used.
The farmer says, "Co'boss, co'boss, co'boss," and the echo comes back.
The wife says, "Moo."            Echo responds.
The baby says, "Goo."            Echo responds.
Baby cries.                      Echo responds.
Farmer says, "Shut up," to baby. Echo responds.
Farmer takes money out of pocket. Realtor, carried away, shouts, "Brother,
  you couldn't do better." Echo shouts, "Brother, you couldn't be done
  better."
Farmer shouts, "What did you say?"
Echo answers, "I said — I mean, what did you say?"
Farmer tears up lease.
Realtor draws gun from his pocket and stalks out in search of the echo.

# #96 Regatta

**PROPS:**
A yacht is represented by a paper funnel (paper cups) strung on cord
  between badminton posts. Cord should be taut. Paper cup carries
  name of a well-known yacht.
A second yacht is similarly prepared.
Toy gun and noise-maker (firecracker)
Bag of salt water taffy kisses, signs, sailor hats, onions

**ACTION:**
Two teams of clowns enter, wearing sailor hats. The names of the yachts
  appear on the hats or uniforms of these teams.

The audience is divided equally into two cheering sections, and signs showing the yacht to be supported are placed in front of each.

Two clowns from each team attempt to blow their yacht along the string from start to finish points. The balance of clowns acts as cheerleaders for their respective sections.

The gun is fired, and action begins. Much blowing, much cheering.

The team that falls behind munches onions to strengthen members' breath. They gradually catch up.

Crowd shouts, "Go, go, go, _____ *(Call out name of yacht)*! One, two, three, four, whom are we for? _____ *(Name of yacht)!*"

Winning team is elected.

Defeated team collapses.

The winning section is showered with candy kisses.

# #97 Ring the Bell

**PROPS:**
A gong fastened to the side of a box and about 30 inches off ground
Balloon attached to length of rubber tubing
Football helmet with fairly large opening on top
Clown mallet
Cigars
Stretcher
Chair

**SCENE:**
Make-believe midway or carnival

**ACTION:**
Chair faces box.

A small clown, wearing the football helmet with the balloon under it and tube leading to his mouth, sits on the chair. He faces the box so that on extending his leg the metal cap of his shoe will ring the bell.

Another clown, the carnival barker, goes to work. "Here you are, folks. Show your strength. Ring the bell and win yourself a big, fat cigar."

He demonstrates how easy it is, repeatedly hitting seated clown lightly on head with hammer. The gong rings every time.

Other clowns gather round. Barker sits on box. Lights a cigar and collects from clowns who take turns trying to ring the bell. Nobody succeeds, although the seated clown's foot jerks slightly.

Clowns try harder and harder. A swelling commences on the seated clown's head and grows alarmingly larger and larger. *(Clown has inflated balloon under his helmet with tube leading to his mouth.)* All gather round in amazement.

If balloon bursts, the clown dies; if not, he faints.

Barker rings gong in alarm. Clown stretcher is brought in. Clown is placed on stretcher *(no signs of life)*.

When ready to carry him off, the barker goes to pick up one end of the stretcher, but the cigar is in his hand. He can't find a place to put it.

Cigar is stuck in the dead man's mouth, and as he is carried off, smoke puffs are noticed.

# #98 Roller Derby I

## PROPS:

Roller skates for all clowns
Brooms (or hockey sticks) for all clowns
Hockey goals
One volleyball

## ACTION:

Clowns are divided into two teams and play hockey, using a volleyball instead of a puck.

Game should be wide open with no goal-keepers.

Ringmaster may serve as referee.

# #99 Roller Derby II

## PROPS:

Several pairs of roller skates
Miniature Ben Hur chariots
Whips
Turning stake or marker

## ACTION:

This is a Ben Hur chariot race.

Three clowns compose a chariot. Two clowns, in front, make a team of horses. The third, behind, is the driver. Only the driver wears roller skates

The miniature chariots are fastened by straps to the driver's ankles so that it appears as though he is standing in a chariot.

A harness of rope or leather runs from the shoulders of the horses around the waist of the driver. Reins lead from driver to the horses' heads.

Driver should have a whip.

Fanfare or roll of drums.

Chariots parade in and make one circle slowly.

Chariots line up. Marker is placed.

Ringmaster announces number of laps.

Race is on.

Winner is about to receive prize from beautiful lady. His team bumps him out of the way, paws the ground and whinnies in front of lady, and then prances off.

# #100 Say *Ouch*

**PROPS:**
Some stage money
A slapstick with pistol cap attached
Paper bag and talcum powder

**ACTION:**
Two clowns argue as to which is the tougher individual.
They show off their muscles.
One clown says, "I'll bet you can't make me say *ouch.*" They bet $5, $10, $100 — a million dollars.
Each time the money is placed on the floor.
One clown takes slapstick and hits the other across the seat as the final bet is made. Pistol cap goes off.
The clown who was hit pays no attention, except to flex his muscles again.
This clown is told to close his eyes. The other takes the slapstick and goes through a few preliminary swings at the other's stomach.
The blow hits where an inflated paper bag containing talcum powder has been placed.
The clown who was hit merely smiles.
The other says, "OK, I give up. You win."
The winner reaches down to pick up the money, but before he gets it he gets the slapstick in the rear.
Jumping in the air, he yells, "Ouch!"
The other picks up the money and walks off.

# #101 Sleeping Hobo

**PROPS:**
Large firecracker
Flash powder
Derby or silk hat, with false crown lined with asbestos

**ACTION:**
Following an act when the clowns are on the floor, the hobo remains in some inconspicuous spot.
He goes to sleep wearing the special hat and sleeps through the next number.
Other clowns discover the sleeping hobo and decide to have some fun.

They tiptoe around him; mimic his loud snores, tickle him, make various animal noises *(barking, mooing, grunting)*, but the hobo sleeps blissfully on.

A large firecracker is produced.

All become very quiet.

One clown lifts false lid of hat and looks in.

He can't see very well, so he beckons to another clown, who brings lighted taper or match on end of stick.

Match inside hat sets off flash powder.

Clowns retreat hurriedly.

Hobo sleeps. Clowns return.

Firecracker is slipped gently into crown of hat.

Signal for match.

Firecracker lit.

Explosion. Clowns fall all over themselves.

Hobo sleeps on.

Another clown, munching a hot dog or a hamburger, has strolled in to see what is going on.

He passes by hobo so that hobo can get a whiff or take a bite, or both.

Hobo revives and follows the clown with the hamburger to the exit.

Other clowns just scratch their heads.

# #102 Surgical Error

## PROPS:
Stretcher, and a table covered with white cloth
Spotlight
White sheet
Rubber gloves for doctor
Number of tins and bottles, marked as indicated below
Sponge, hammer, saw, knives
Valise for doctor's kit
Flashlight, matches, camera and flash, cauliflower
Balloon, waterwings, large dice, tape measure
Clown hammer
Sign: OPENED BY MISTAKE

## CHARACTERS:
Clown doctor
Two other clowns (assistants)
One sick clown with fake stomach (half a small barrel)

## ACTION:
Operating table is placed in center of room under spotlight. Sick clown is brought in on stretcher by the assistants and laid on the table. White sheet, with a slit in the center for expediting the operation which is to follow, is thrown over him.

Lights go out, except spotlight. Roll of drums.

Doctor enters. All bow.

Doc looks situation over as clowns look over his shoulders.

Doc shakes head dubiously.

Doc takes a sponge out of bag and calls for ether. Clowns hand him a tin marked "Either." This has no effect on patient, who groans away.

Doc calls for chloroform. Clown finds cauliflower in bag. Patient sits up and sucks sponge. A bottle marked "Garlic" puts the subject to sleep. Patient comes to and is hit on head with clown hammer.

Doc sharpens knives. Assistants shudder. Patient is so tough that knife won't enter. Nor will a saw. Stomach has zipper opening which one of the clowns now pulls.

Bright red balloon appears, grows and bursts *(tube to patient's mouth)*.

Doc rubs hands as he looks in, exclaiming, "Cancer." He takes out one tin can. Clown looks in and says "Tumor." Takes out two cans.

Waterwings daubed with paint — spots on lungs. Large dice — gallstones. Tape measure — tapeworm.

Doc takes flashlight to inspect job. It doesn't work. Lights match, which is inserted in false stomach, and at same time camera release is worked to explode flash bulb.

Throws in flashlight, sponge, a couple of tins. Pulls zipper.

Hangs sign: OPENED BY MISTAKE. *(Lights out.)*

# #103 Swat Fest

**PROPS:**

Two barrels                                    Two wands
Set of boxing gloves

**ACTION:**

The barrels are placed on end about one foot apart. Clowns, wearing boxing gloves, take their positions, one on each barrel.

The clown wins who knocks his opponent off the barrel.

After the first bout, "best two out of three" is announced.

Clowns take positions again.

Accomplices who have remained hidden in the barrels now extend wands through bung holes and push and parry in an attempt to help clowns on top. Of course, this makes the top position more precarious.

For a deciding third round, pillows may be substituted for boxing gloves.

Note: The pillow fight may be used by two clowns, straddling a high bar on other horizontal pole.

# #104 Swat the Rattle

*(A well-known gym game that becomes hilarious when played by clowns.)*

**PROPS:**
A blindfold
A 10-foot length of sash cord, and a two-foot length of sash cord
A swatter
A bell or rattle

**ACTION:**
Clowns form a circle.
Two clowns go into the center. One is blindfolded, and the other is given the bell or rattle. The blindfolded clown is given the swatter.
The blindfolded clown chants:

"Tinkle, tinkle, little bell,
I can't hear you very well."

Then the other clown rings the bells, and guided by the noise, the blindfolded clown attempts to swat the other. Naturally, the clown with the bell assumes ridiculous positions in order to avoid being hit.
Two more clowns take the center, and this time the game is made more interesting by showing them the two-foot length of rope and explaining that each will hold one end of the rope with the free hand.
Change players again with same explanation, but when one clown is blindfolded, substitute the 10-foot length of rope so that the bell may be rung under the blindfolded clown's nose but the other can retreat quietly to a safe distance. Much wild swinging.
Finally, the blindfolded clown gets wise and he hauls in on the rope until he can give the other a good biff.
Clown policeman chases off all.

# #105 A Timely Affair

**PROPS:**
Some stage money
A number of alarm clocks, preferably small

**ACTION:**
Before the show commences, the alarm clocks are planted on obliging customers, in purses, handbags, parcels and pockets.
These people are given some stage money and are told they will be arrested sometime during the show for what they have just been given, and that the money is to pay the fine. They should not know what the article is.
All the alarm clocks are set to go off at intermission. Two or three acts before

intermission, the clown cop comes running in and excitedly whispers to the ringmaster.

The ringmaster informs the audience that Blank's Jewelry shop has been robbed and it is suspected that the thief or thieves are hiding here.

Cop looks searchingly through audience as show goes on and then leaves.

After the next act he returns and again whispers to ringmaster, who announces that they now know that some valuable timepieces have been stolen.

If there is the opportunity, clown cop comes back and the people are told that it is alarm clocks which are missing.

During intermission the alarms begin to go off and the cop has a busy time making arrests and collecting fines.

If the cooperation of a friendly, real cop can be obtained, he could make-believe that he is arresting the president for possessing bogus money.

One of the clowns could have a clock in the stomach of his costume. On complaining to the ringmaster about butterflies in his stomach, the ringmaster could say that that noise was usually in the clown's head.

# #106 Track Meet

## PROPS:

Several inflated balloons including the type obtainable from the Weather Bureau which are most difficult to break
Two chairs
Two relay batons
Starting pistol
Signs: START, FINISH, TURN

## ACTION:

Clowns come running on and go through the business of warming up.

Official starter *(clown)* blows whistle and clowns form two teams facing chairs at opposite end of hall. The TURN sign is placed there.

START and FINISH signs are placed on line in front of teams.

Balloons are placed under chairs.

Starter raises gun.

A clown shouts, "What do we do?"

Starter puts a balloon on each chair and demonstrates by pantomime that they are to run to the chair, sit down hard on the balloon, and when it breaks they are to run back, giving the baton to the next runner.

The race is on. One runner falls flat, and the other gets a head start. Much consternation, but the one with the head start finds his balloon doesn't break easily, while the other's does.

The starter sees that a balloon is always on hand for the next runner, and if one fails to break after a few attempts, he should have a pin handy.

Much of the fun is in the antics of the clowns in trying to burst the hard-to-burst balloons.

Winning team can be given a goofy trophy, or they can all gang up on the starter, pushing the balloons inside the seat of his pants and, holding him by the wrists and ankles, bounce him off the floor.

# #107 Two Rabbits

## PROPS:
A cart
A crate with open sides covered with wire netting
Any quantity of rabbits

## ACTION:
The pattern of action is the same as for "Ice for Mrs. Smaltz."
A clown circles the floor, pulling a cart on which is a crate containing two rabbits.
The clown inquires en route, "Did anybody here leave these two rabbits in Mr. _____'s office?"
After the next act the same clown returns and repeats the rabbit act. He has the same inquiry, making sure to say, "two rabbits." However, there are four rabbits in the crate, but since the clown never looks at the crate, he is none the wiser.
Next time, clown goes a little slower with his heavier wagon.
And so on. More rabbits each trip.
Clown may nibble at a carrot between announcements.

# #108 Under the Spreading Chestnut Tree

## PROPS:
A park bench                                     Streetlight or spotlight

## CHARACTERS:
Two comedians
One clown who is covered with branches to resemble a tree

## ACTION:
Lights out, while bench is placed and clown takes position behind it.
Two comedians enter after spotlight comes on and sit on the bench under the tree.
The two comedians exchange jokes in deadpan fashion.
The tree is convulsed, each time, with silent laughter. Its limbs shake and it bends nearly double.
After a few stories the comedians begin to notice the tree.
Finally, one of the comedians says, "I wonder what kind of a tree this is."
To which the tree replies, in a deep bass voice, "Why, don't you know?

I'm a *chestnut* tree. An *old chestnut* tree."

# #109 Under the Underwear

Instead of wearing clown suits, two clowns are attired in long, loose-fitting underwear, the more colorful, the better.

The clowns are provided with a good supply of inflated balloons. These should be all shapes and sizes.

It is announced that this is a contest to see which clown can stuff inside his suit of underwear the greatest number of balloons in three minutes.

A clown, or the ringmaster, may give the starting and stopping signals, and other clowns may keep score on a blackboard with the contestants enrolled according to the color of their suits.

Clowns should walk off as though floating on air.

# #110 Weight Lifting

**PROPS:**

A dummy barbell made of wood to look like the real thing

**ACTION:**

The fake barbell is brought out with other weight-lifting equipment and stays on the floor for a regular demonstration by competent lifters.

After their act, and before the equipment is carried off, two clowns enter. These should be the largest and smallest clowns in the group.

The large clown flexes his muscles, to the admiration of the small clown. Large clown makes signs indicating the amateurishness of the former performers.

The large clown, who is wearing a little hat, takes deep breath and manages to lift the large dummy weight to his knees. Small clown turns his back to laugh.

Large clown wipes his brow. Takes off his hat and places it on one end of the weight.

When he lifts again, only the end without the hat comes up. Hat is put on other end. Same result.

Clown puts hat back on his head and prepares for one last desperate effort. He gives a terrific tug in bent-knee position.

Nothing happens, except clown's fingers are so firmly curled around the bar he can't release them.

Small clown pries off fingers one at a time, and on being released the big clown staggers around the floor in ape fashion.

Small clown picks up bar in one hand and walks off.

# #111 What a Nerve!
## (At the Dentist's)

**PROPS:**
Dentist's chair
Assortment of tools and drills (brace and bit)
A large hollow tooth made of papier mâché, with hinged top
A tame white mouse
Sheets and bandages

**CHARACTERS:**
Clown dentist wearing sheet or white uniform
Female clown assistant (not essential)
Clown patient, jaw swathed in rolls of bandage

**ACTION:**
Dentist and assistant busy themselves about the office putting tools in
    order, looking at old X-ray plates, and so on.
Groans are heard. *(Can be dubbed in over P.A.)*
Clown with toothache enters slowly and painfully.
Pantomimes before dentist about tooth.
Business of taking off unending bandages.
Patient is put in chair.
Anæsthetic. Then much drilling and much groaning.
Dentist tries pliers and monkey wrenches for size.
Under cover of sheet dentist extracts tooth, which was hidden under
    patient's shirt.
Patient is immediately better.
He congratulates dentist.
Patient asks if he can see the nerve of the tooth.
Dentist asks, "You want to see the nerve?"
Clown nods.
Dentist opens hinged top of tooth, and the tame white mouse crawls out.
Patient takes nerve *(mouse)* and exits, but in so doing he walks once
    around the room and very close to the audience so that he can show
    off the nerve.

# #112 Woof! Woof!

**PROPS:**
A live dog that will bark on command
Stage money

**ACTION:**
Two clowns enter. Owner has dog on leash. Owner boasts about his unusually

intelligent dog.

Other clown is dubious but willing to be shown.

Dog does a couple of simple tricks. Owner claims that dog can talk. Other refuses to believe. Owner backs down a bit and admits that, at least, the dog can speak his own name.

Clowns bet millions of dollars.

Second clown asks, "And what is the dog's name?"

The owner says, "Woof."

The dog says, "Woof."

And owner and dog walk off with the money.

Note: There are toy dogs that bark, and it may be necessary for the owner to secrete one of these under his suit so that a squeeze at the right moment will produce the *woof* in case the dog fails.

# #113 Yes, No Banana

## PROPS:

Two chairs

A board about five feet long and two feet wide

Three felt hats of the same color

A banana

## ACTION:

A board is laid across the backs of two chairs. On the board are the three felt hats.

A clown takes his place behind the board and, producing a banana, he puts it under one of the hats.

He then shifts the hats about and attempts to guess which hat the banana is under. If he guesses right he shows much glee; if wrong, he is greatly distressed.

Another clown comes in and watches proceedings.

First clown shifts hats again. He decides on one hat. Second clown points to another. They are both wrong. Bets are now made that the visiting clown cannot select the hat hiding the banana.

First clown places the banana under a hat. Hats are moved about so that all the audience can follow the hat with the banana under it.

Second clown is asked to make his choice. He selects the hat which everyone knows covers the fruit.

First clown hesitates. He asks second clown if he is sure he doesn't want to make another choice. Second clown remains firm.

First clown picks up the hat, pressing down so that the banana is picked up, too.

First clown also picks up the money, places the hat and banana on his head, and walks off.

Second clown looks under the remaining two hats. Realizing he has been had, he lets out a shout and goes chasing after first clown.

# #114 Your Picture in Ten Seconds

## PROPS:
Clown camera (may be real press camera)
Red and black greasepaints
Two lollypops
Two cheap mirrors inside separate envelopes
Small stool

## CHARACTERS:
Photographer                      Assistant
A boy accomplice

## ACTION:
Photographer and assistant enter with equipment. Accomplice has been seated in audience.

Photographer announces, "Your photo in only 10 seconds. Regular charge $1. Introductory offer, no charge, absolutely nothing. Who would like his picture taken? Boys are our specialty. Who'll be the first?" Accomplice comes forward.

Photographer and assistant do a straightforward job of taking the picture. The lad is posed on the stool, first facing the camera, then profile. A lollypop is placed in his mouth, his hair is smoothed, eyebrows, too. When the picture has been taken, the boy is presented with an envelope containing a mirror.

The photographer now goes after a victim, and a second offer of a free picture is given. With the lollypop for bait, a victim can be expected.

The photographer and assistant repeat the routine, but this act takes longer and more attention is given the subject. Both photographer and assistant secretly apply greasepaint to thumb and index fingers of one hand and do a job on the boy as they turn his face one way and then another.

Photographer and assistant find business is very bad after this. They pack up and leave in disgust.

CHAPTER 7

# Clown Acts with Constructed Equipment

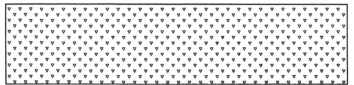

The main thing to remember about equipment for clown acts is that it must be highly visible to the audience. A flit gun, razor, scissors, keys and other accessories that clowns may carry must be larger than life. A bottle must have a big label. A hot dog or a hamburger must be large enough to be recognized instantly. Lettering on signs or labels must be legible to the audience.

In clowning, nothing is left to the imagination. The humor is *obvious* humor, and equipment plays a big part in explaining the act to the audience. Whether equipment is made in the agency workshop, borrowed or bought, make sure that the audience can see it and identify it instantly.

# #115 Art

**PROPS:**
Two large picture frames, containing nothing but paper, are set on easels
Siren
A clown Black Maria or police wagon
Half-dozen chairs
Butterfly net, flit gun
Sign: THE NUT HOUSE — A SCREWY HOME FOR LOOSE NUTS

**CHARACTERS:**
Clown 1                          Clown 2
Other clowns

**ACTION:**
*(Pictures are placed in a row. Chairs are set as for art gallery display, facing pictures. A clown sits on a chair admiring pictures. He goes into raptures with appropriate contortions. Other clowns drift in and sit beside Clown 1. They gaze in proper bewilderment at the clown and the alleged pictures. Clown 2 taps Clown 1 on the shoulder and points at white sheet.)*

**Clown 2:**
What's that picture?

**Clown 1:**
That's the Israelites crossing the Red Sea. *(All look again.)*

**Clown 2:**
But where are the Israelites?

**Clown 1:**
They've crossed over.

**Clown 2:**
Then where are the Egyptians?

**Clown 1:**
They haven't arrived yet.

**Clown 2:**
But where is the Red Sea?

**Clown 1:**
Stupid! The sea is rolled back.

**Clown 2:**
*(Points to second picture.)* What's that?

**Clown 1:**
That's a polar bear sitting in a snow bank eating marshmallows.

*(All clowns, except Clown 1, steal away on tiptoe. A siren sounds offstage, and clowns rush in with clown police wagon, which is marked with the sign: THE NUT HOUSE, etc. One clown carries a butterfly net, and another a flit gun or insect spray. The art student is picked up and deposited in the wagon, and all exit.)*

# #116 Astronomical Adventures

**CHARACTERS:**
The Professor — top hat, morning suit, mustache, large horn-rimmed glasses
Volunteer — a clown

**PROPS:**
A six-foot telescope made of galvanized tin, on a six-foot pedestal
Other props in skit shown in bold italics

**ACTION:**
**Professor:**
Ladies and gentlemen, it gives me great pleasure to introduce to you this evening this mammoth telescopic telescope. I shall say a word in describing

this invention to you, after which I will endeavor to give a practical demonstration which will prove that this instrument is second to none in size, beauty and power.

Through this instrument I have been able to prove that the planets are planted, that the sun is hotter by day than by night, that the North Star may be found in the north and the Southern Cross in the south. This telescope has detected the polar star, the polar bear, the tadpole and the polecat, the clothesline pole, a few voting polls and numerous telephone poles in _____ *(nearby town or part of city)*.

In this instrument, ladies and gentlemen, I employ the use of four lenses, one concave, one convex, one circular and one degenerated. With the aid of this combination of lenses it is possible to see a few feet or beyond a million light years.

If Newton, Kepler, Galileo, Copernicus or any of the other famous probers into the unknown regions above us, were here tonight, they would undoubtedly give to me the credit of having discovered the most remarkable invention of the age.

Therefore, ladies and gentlemen, if there is anyone in this audience tonight sufficiently interested and informed in the study of astronomy, will he please step forward at this time, and I shall endeavor to prove to all and sundry the remarkable merits of this delicate telescope.

*(The Volunteer steps forward and is welcomed by the Professor, who is somewhat skeptical as to the Volunteer's qualifications. The Volunteer gives the telescope the once-over, admiring the pictures of the constellations painted on it. The Volunteer seats himself on a **chair** at the eyepiece of the instrument. A **ladder** is brought out and placed at the opposite end. The Professor, with **club bag** in hand, climbs the ladder. He is at the open end of the telescope and is considerably higher than the Volunteer. The Professor proceeds to display various constellations. In the club bag he has a **dipper**, a **frying pan**, a **kewpie doll**, a **teddy bear** and a **bottle of milk**.)*

**Volunteer:**
*(After each showing)* W-o-n-d-e-r-f-u-l, m-a-g-n-i-f-i-c-e-n-t!

*(He continually asks to see Venus, but the Professor puts him off. Finally the Kewpie Doll is shown, to the exuberant delight of Volunteer — wolf whistle.)*

**Volunteer:**
*(Interrupts.)* Professor, Professor, I see the moon.

*(The Professor explains that he can't see the moon because it is behind a cloud. The Volunteer persists, so the Professor gets down from the ladder to take a look.)*

**Professor:**
You dope, that isn't the moon, that's the hole in Mr. _____'s

haircut.

*(The Volunteer gets the idea he can fool the Professor and asks to see the Milky Way. The Professor puts him off, showing other constellations including the horizon. For this he pretends to take a hair from his head and stretches it across the mouth of the telescope. The Volunteer suggests that the horizon must be in Africa. The Professor asks why.)*

**Volunteer:**
Because I see two elephants walking across it.

*(For the finale the Professor grants the Volunteer's wish to see the Milky Way. Standing in front of the telescope and holding the bottle so that it can be seen by the audience but not by the Volunteer, he removes the stopper.)*

**Professor:**
Are you sure you want to see the Milky Way?

**Volunteer:**
Oh, yes, I do! *(This is repeated.)*

**Professor:**
OK. Here's the Milky Way.

*(He pours the contents of the milk bottle down the telescope funnel. The Volunteer holds his position, getting the contents in the face. The Professor makes a quick exit, and the Volunteer chases him off, spouting milk as he goes.)*

# #117 Barbershop

**PROPS:**
Large wooden razor, razor strop, large sheet
Tin of pressurized whipping cream, labeled SHAVING CREAM
Glass of water
Various ads for hair tonic
Stage ears and nose
Electric fan (not necessary)
Huge pair of scissors (lawn shears)
Barber's chair or substitute

**CHARACTERS:**
Clown barber                          Clown customer
Third clown

**ACTION:**
The barbershop having been established, the barber enters.
"Shave and a haircut. Best and cheapest in town. Who wants a shave? Doesn't

anyone need a shave?"

Clown wearing false nose and ears comes in, stroking his chin. Barber captures him and puts him in chair. Sheet is tied so tightly around the victim's neck that he chokes. Barber revives him with glass of water in face. While victim splutters, the barber drinks what is left in glass.

Business of applying shaving cream *(whipped cream)* which should be done generously.

Barber strops razor, and yanks a hair out of victim's head to test razor. Not satisfactory. More stropping, more testing. The victim becomes more and more irritated.

Shaving commences. Barber is not too careful about where he whips the lather off the razor.

Barber accidentally cuts off one fake ear and throws it on the floor. Victim hollers. Barber shoots his mouth full of cream.

This is repeated for other ear and nose.

During any part of the scene above a third clown may enter carrying an electric fan with cord attached to electric outlet. As he gawks at victim, the fan is turned on, causing havoc with cream.

Victim discovers he likes taste of cream. Starts scooping it off his face and eating it. Barber does likewise. When this monkey business is over, the victim is asked if he would like a haircut. He nods his head, but on seeing the huge pair of scissors held by the barber, he flees, with the barber in pursuit.

# #118 Billiard Game

## PROPS:
A small billiard table
Balls of rubber, painted, one of them white
Cues, cue chalk
A cord, strung between two upright poles, and 10 doughnuts placed in center of cord as counters

## ACTION:
Table and counters are placed in central location. A spotlight could substitute for usual billiard table lighting.

Two players enter carrying and chalking cues. They play a snooker type of game.

Each time a ball is pocketed it is respotted, and the player makes quite a show of moving a counter.

Two or more other clowns become spectators, stationing themselves conveniently at the ends of the counting device.

As doughnuts are moved from center to ends, the spectators *(clowns)* become tempted and eat the doughnuts nearest them.

The players fail to notice the disappearing counters until none is left.

Players chase clown spectators around the pool table with much brandishing of cues and some paddling.

The bad clowns scoop up the rubber billiard balls and pelt the players off the floor. *(Clowns could have a few extra balls in their pockets.)*

# #119 Bull Thrower

**PROPS:**

A bull (two clowns under a blanket, brown overalls, face of bull made of papier mâché)

Red ribbon, red cloth or blanket

Bell

Sword

Auto bulb horn

**ACTION:**

Clown toreador enters after introduction and flourish of trumpets.

He bows. Tests sword. Waves to the pretty girls.

Roar of bull is heard offstage.

Bull thunders in. Red ribbons around his neck and bell under chin.

Bull comes to a stop, telescoping.

Bull bows, scratches leg.

Tries to find seat in bleachers among ladies.

Bull and toreador now face each other and glare. Toreador waves blanket.

They circle one another, first one way, then the other. Bull gets dizzy and sits down. Toreador sits down and waits.

Waltz music is heard. Bull gets up and dances about. Wants to dance with toreador.

Toreador sticks bull with sword. Old auto horn sounds inside bull *(mortally wounded, almost).*

Bull and toreador begin circling again.

Toreador gets his head enveloped in the blanket. Bull charges toreador.

Toreador chases bull offstage with sword used as slapstick.

Toreador returns for a bow. He bows often.

Bull returns on the run to catch toreador in one of his bows.

# #120 A Case of Misunderstanding

**PROPS:**

Sign: GENERAL NUISANCE

Desk, three electric buttons or buzzers on surface

Cowbell, whistle, auto horn, aspirin bottle

Gun and blank cartridge

**CHARACTERS:**

Clown dressed as general          Clown dressed as private

**ACTION:**

General is seated at desk, sign on top of which indicates GENERAL NUISANCE.

Much twirling of mustache, reading of orders and the like.

General presses button #1. Cowbell sounds offstage *(or accomplice hidden under table rings bell)*. No one responds. General shows impatience.

Presses button #2. Whistle sounds. No one responds. General thumps chest with fists. Pushes button #3. Auto horn sounds. No one responds. General stands and thumps table. He presses three buttons simultaneously. Sounds from all contraptions are heard, and private rushes in.

Business of saluting.

General: "Private _____, I want you to take my horse and have him shod. That is all."

Business of saluting and heel-clicking.

Private withdraws. He returns immediately with a package containing a big bottle labeled ASPIRIN, which he places on the table. Private withdraws.

General opens parcel and showing bottle, reads note: "This will cure your cold."

General stands up, reads label. Looks mystified, then suddenly clasps hands to head in agonized anticipation.

Shot is heard offstage.

General collapses, sitting on buttons. Bell, whistle and horn all sound. *(Lights out.)*

# #121 Cave Man Stuff

**PROPS:**

Leopard skin or imitation leotards, or prehistoric costumes of burlap for three people, two male, one female

Two prehistoric clubs made from burlap and stuffed with cloth and paper

Imitation campfire and red light underneath

**ACTION:**

Lights are dimmed. Campfire is placed.

Clown 1, carrying club, and followed by his woman, enters and sits by fire. *(Tomtom or other music may be provided.)*

Clown does a number of stunts to impress his woman — cartwheels, balances, flips. He does a lot of posing, flexing muscles, clicking his heels.

He thumps his chest with one hand, emitting a vigorous and lusty yell. He thumps himself with the other fist and just about collapses with a hollow cough.

Music changes to seductive South Seas melody.

The woman *(male clown)* rises and performs a hip-wiggling dance. *(She wears a wig which is held in place by a strap that goes around the head and under the chin.)*

While she is dancing, a third cave man clown sneaks in and circles round with his club in a threatening position.

A fight follows, and the amount of punishment absorbed by the two male combatants is terrific.

Female cowers in shadows.

One male is knocked out.

The victor taps the woman on the head, and she keels over.

She is seized by the hair *(strap)* and dragged off.

# #122 Census 1975

## PROPS:
Crate containing three chickens
Dish towel
Plate
Large cardboard box on special wooden frame and on casters, which should be about two-thirds the size of a single horse trailer
Door frame and a door that will open and close

## ACTION:
The chickens in the crate and the box imitating a horse trailer *(straw sticking out)* are placed in center of floor. The door prop is placed near the exit.

It is announced that this is the year 1975 *(or other year)* and after many years the _____ political party has finally come into power. They have decided to take a census of the people, and rather than give them bacon and eggs for every breakfast, they will give a chicken where the wife is boss in the home and a horse where the husband is boss. Let us now observe the census-taker at work.

Clown Census-Taker enters. He wears glasses, has a portfolio, notepad and pencil.

He circles back to door and knocks.

Male clown answers with plate and dish towel in hand.

Census-Taker just looks. No words are spoken.

Census-Taker goes to crate, gets chicken, and hands it to clown at door.

Door closes; Census-Taker walks in circle and comes back to door. Knocks.

Clown wearing wig and dress answers.

### Census-Taker:
May I inquire as to who is the head of this house?

### Lady:
I am the ruler of this house.

*(She gets a chicken. Third door. Knock is answered by big clown. Same*

*question is put.)*

**Clown:**
I'm the boss in this house.

**Census-Taker:**
In that case you are entitled to a horse. Do you want a white one or a black one?

**Clown:**
Just a minute, please. *(Clown disappears inside house and returns.)* We'll have a white one.

*(Census-Taker gives him a chicken. Lights out.)*

# #123 Chariot Race

**PROPS:**
Three ash cans (one of which has no bottom), on casters
Rope traces and reins
Markers for course
Carrots or apples or shock of oats

**ACTION:**
Each chariot has a driver who stands inside ash can, and there is a horse for each chariot.
Chariots line up.
Starter raises three fingers to indicate three laps.
The start. They're off.
The specially prepared chariot lags behind on the first lap, at the end of which one or two clowns distract the leading entries by using apples or carrots for bait.
Lead chariots stop, and third gets a good lead. Other two finally take off in pursuit.
At close of second lap the leading chariot is diverted and comes to a full stop, the others continuing on.
The stopped horse won't go, so the driver drops the reins, picks up ash can by handles, and raising the chariot so he can run, takes off in hot pursuit.
The horseless chariot hits the finish line as closely as possible to be a winner; trips and rolls sideways along the floor inside the rolling chariot.
Chariot driver is pushed unceremoniously off the track by stagehands.

# #124 Cooking Lesson

**SCENE:**
Represents a kitchen. Table with box under it contains equipment required for cooking lesson.

A stove with back removed is standing against a false wall. There is a radio, ironing board, an iron, some things to be ironed, and a professionally prepared cake (hidden).

**ACTION:**
Radio is playing music. *(Connect to P.A. system offstage.)* Clown is ironing.

Music is interrupted and voice says, "I suppose many a man is home tonight doing the chores that belong to his wife while she is out having a good time at the Cat's Paw Bridge Club. *(Clown nods head.)* Well, how many of you have secretly desired to bake a cake that would put any of hers to shame? I'll bet you have, and I'm going to tell you how to do it. It's, oh, so easy, and you can't miss. Are you ready?"

Clown stops ironing and follows directions.

*(If small cloth is left under iron on fireproof cover and iron is actually attached, this will add to scene.)*

"Take a clean white bowl." *(A battered old 10-quart pail.)*

"Put in two cups of flour." *(Measure with shaving mug.)*

"Some salt, enough to catch a partridge."

"A cup of sugar." *(Lump sugar.)*

"A pint of liquid, and stir slowly." *(Clown turns himself.)*

"Now beat two eggs together." *(Clown is confused, but finally puts an egg in each hand and smacks them together.)*

"A little peppermint." *(Take Life-Saver out of mouth.)*

"Some raisins and nuts." *(Nuts go in unshelled.)*

"And a little peel adds real flavor." *(Banana peel.)*

"Now pour in a pan and place in oven for two minutes."

This is done and music comes back on.

Clown goes back to ironing. His back is to stove.

The accomplice behind the false wall removes the cooking mess and lights some oily rags or anything that will cause the oven to smoke.

Some small firecrackers are let off in the oven.

From the rear, unseen by audience, a beautiful cake with lighted candles is placed in the oven.

Music is interrupted. Voice says that the cake should now be ready.

Clown victoriously removes cake and marches off, holding cake over-head.

# #125 Dead-Eye Dick

**PROPS:**
Pistol                                        Gun

129

Crackers

Balloons

Old crockery

Specially prepared box

Cigarettes

Candles

Hammer

**ACTION:**

The ringmaster announces that the show has been most fortunate in pro-
curing the services of one of the really big shots of our time: Dead-Eye
Dick — dead in one eye and can't see out of the other.

Fanfare. Entry of Dead-Eye Dick, dressed in cowboy costume. Blank cartridges
in gun, pistol, or both.

Dead-Eye shoots from all angles. He shoots between his legs, back to
target using a mirror — he even stands on his head while shooting.

1. Clown holds soda cracker between his fingers. Dead-Eye fires, and
   cracker crumbles. Clown pinches cracker between fingers.
2. Clown smokes cigarette. As he puffs smoke, Dead-Eye fires, and clown
   turns cigarette back inside his mouth. Dead-Eye fires again, and cigarette
   reappears.
3. Stunts with special box: Box holds small accomplice who sits behind
   a black screen, unseen by audience. Balloons and old cups hang by
   string from top of box and in front of screen. There is a shelf holding
   candles.

Dead-Eye shoots the balloons as different colors are called. He shoots
red when green is called.

Ringmaster explains he is color-blind.

Dead-Eye shoots out the candle flames with the help of the accomplice
who lines up a straw or tube with the flame.

Dead-Eye now shoots the cups. Accomplice has a hammer with which
he strikes the cups.

He misses the last one, rolling out on the floor with hammer in hand.

Lights out. *(Note: Dead-Eye's slow bullet may also be featured — slight
delay from time of firing to the breaking of the target.)*

# #126 Egg-Zactly

**PROPS:**

A stepladder

A long telescope made of shaped tin and mounted

A basket of eggs — two real ones, the others imitation, or blown (There
must be at least one blown egg included.)

**ACTION:**

Telescope is set up in middle of floor with stepladder leading to larger end.

The clown promoter announces, "See all the stars you want for egg-zactly
one dime."

First customer enters and pays his dime and sits down with eye to small end of telescope.

He is asked what star he wants to see.

Regardless of what star is named, the customer is told that he will get egg-zactly what he asked for.

The basket of eggs sits on the shelf of the ladder, and at the right moment the promoter reaches into the basket and selects a genuine egg.

The egg is allowed to run down the shoot inside the telescope, and as the customer sees it coming, he shifts his forehead to the "eye" of the scope and receives the full treatment.

The customer is succeeded by another one, and the stunt is repeated.

First customer returns but is not recognized by the promoter.

Same deal is made, and customer sits down.

This time the promoter substitutes a blown egg for the real thing, and this, the knowing customer catches tenderly and neatly as it drops through the hole.

Customer lets out a menacing "ha-ha" as he advances toward the promoter, who hastily retreats from the ladder.

Promoter gets himself cornered where he takes shelter in the audience. The irate customer draws back his arm and throws the blown egg into the crowd.

# #127 Elephant Act

## PROPS:
Elephant frame of wood and wire to be worn on shoulders of two boys
Bag of peanuts
Sign — one side reading: 300 LBS., other side reading: 300 OZ.
Inner tube from auto tire

## CHARACTERS:
The elephant                                    Trainer
Clowns

## ACTION:
Trainer enters, followed by trained elephant. Then come the clowns, who link on to elephant's tail and each other.

One of these clowns has the inner tube inflated under his costume and around his stomach. He wears the sign on the side reading "300 LBS."

Clowns form a circle around the elephant and trainer, and the elephant goes through routine.

Tells age by stamping foot.

Tells age of young lady in audience, but doesn't stop stamping until prodded a few times by trainer.

Wiggles ears *(using wire attachments)*.

Front end gets peanuts for good performance. Rear end shifts around until able to reach out a hand and take peanut out of trainer's pocket.

131

Elephant sits on chair.

Balances on one chair.

Walks over clowns, who show considerable fear.

Elephant points out prettiest woman in audience.

Asked to point out ugliest man, the elephant points at trainer.

Clowns now line up on floor in prone positions for elephant to demonstrate a hurdle race.

Elephant starts out on the double and grows more tired with each hurdle. The fat clown is last, and the elephant just gets over him and sits down on clown.

Much consternation. Fat clown is being squeezed to death. Others gather round, trying to lift off elephant.

One clown unscrews valve in inner tube.

Clown deflates. Elephant rises and exits.

Clowns follow, and the sign on the former fat clown is flipped over to read: 300 OZ.

# #128 Elopement

## PROPS:

Gym mats

A scene to represent a house with an upstairs window

A number of suitcases, a bird cage, a rolling pin

A stepladder, reinforced so that it may be rocked backward and forward by a performer standing on the top platform (Vertical hand rails will help.)

## CHARACTERS:

The girl                                    The lover

The girl's father                      (All may be clowns.)

## SCENE:

Mats are placed lengthwise below window.

## ACTION:

Clown enters carrying ladder.

He places this below the window, sideways to the wall, so that the ladder may be rocked to and fro below the window.

Clown whistles. Girl appears above. Clown climbs ladder, and they embrace. She disappears momentarily. She returns and gives him suitcase and he takes it down to the ground. Repeat with more suitcases, bird cage, rolling pin and other parcels.)

The last time up the clown is getting pretty teetery.

Instead of the girl appearing at the window, it is the father, who strikes the clown with a stuffed baton.

Window is closed, blind pulled, and clown starts rocking the ladder.

Eventually, ladder and clown fall to the mat, where he does a roll as the girl screams. *(Lights out.)*

# #129 Epidemic

**PROPS:**

Two or three flit guns

Several boxes of facial tissue

Hot water bottle, blanket, thermometer

Large bottle marked ASPIRIN and filled with checkers painted white

Red Cross wagon (This can be built like an ice cream wagon. Should be on wheels or a coaster wagon. Red Cross signs should be on all sides, and words: WE FIGHT COLDS.)

A siren or gong

Giant syringe

**ACTION:**

**Ringmaster:**

Ladies and gentlemen, you have all heard it said that something is not to be sneezed at, but believe me the next act is well worth sneezing at. Therefore, I am going to ask you to perform with me a giant sneeze. When I give the sign, this side will say, "Hish." This said, "Hash." This side, "Hosh." This side, after the sneeze, "Gesundheit."

Ringmaster has each side practice separately, then all together, three times in succession.

After the final sneeze a siren is heard offstage, and there is much clamoring as clowns rush in with the Red Cross wagon.

Clowns with squirt guns spray the audience with perfumed water.

Other clowns pass out facial tissues and occasionally blow the nose.

Clown with aspirins drops bottle on the way in, and tablets roll on floor. He picks them up and tries to get members in the audience to swallow one.

Another clown has selected someone in the audience whom he attempts to bundle up with blanket and hot water bottle. The thermometer *(giant size)* is thrust in this person's mouth.

After a couple of minutes a shout is heard as another clown rushes in with the giant syringe.

All take fright and run off, followed by clown with syringe.

# #130 Freedom of Speech

**PROPS:**

Police wagon or Black Maria (This should be a large framework structure with the front end resting on a wagon which is the engine hood and in which the driver sits. Wagon should have steering wheel and gong.)

A number of clown policeman's billies

One red rubber balloon

A soap box

## ACTION:

Clown parade carrying various signs.

Agitator mounts soapbox and gives a political speech or recites the alphabet excitedly and with gestures. Clowns cheer and applaud.

Clown policeman discovers gathering and blows whistle. Gong and siren and other whistles are heard. Police wagon rushes in. *(It has no wheels except those on cart. The framework is carried by stagehands who have handle grips on inside frame, and they simply run and carry and push car.)*

The driver is a clown policeman, and he and other policeman from inside the police wagon pour out and use billies on those in the gathering.

All are hustled into the wagon. Action should be fast and furious with much wild swinging. If one or two clowns in the gathering are dressed as women, so much the funnier.

Wagon takes off with all aboard except one cop who tries to get in the back door. As the wagon exits, one clown is left on his back on the floor as though he had fallen through the bottom of the cart.

Policeman accidentally steps on this clown's stomach on the way.

A red balloon appears in the mouth of this remaining clown.

It swells and swells until it bursts.

Clown runs off.

# #131 George and the Dragon

A paper-covered framework is built to depict the front of an inn.

Over the door is a sign: GEORGE AND DRAGON INN.

There is a second-story window which is reached from a ladder on the rear side of the structure.

Lights go out one at a time to indicate the lateness of the hour.

Snoring is heard. An illuminated moon rises.

A hobo clown enters. He is obviously hungry, rubbing his stomach, searching his kit for food.

He spies the inn and pantomimes reading out the sign. The clown knocks. No one answers. He raises a horrible din.

Finally, an old lady wearing a bed cap sticks her head out of the window.

**Lady:**
*(Crankily)* What do you want?

**Clown:**
Please, ma'am, I'm hungry. Could you spare a poor man a scrap of food?

**Lady:**
I should say not. *(She withdraws.)*

*(Clown lies down to sleep but can't get comfortable. He again knocks, and*

*again the lady answers.)*

**Lady:**
Well, what is it this time?

**Clown:**
If you please, have you got a bed to spare?

**Lady:**
Certainly not. Good night!

*(She again withdraws. The clown thinks as he walks around in a circle, scratching his head. He stops and rereads the sign. With a pleased expression, he knocks once more.)*

**Lady:**
*(Reappearing)* Well, what is it this time?

**Clown:**
If you please, ma'am, could I speak to George?

# #132 Ghosts

**PROPS:**
Two wooden tombstones, large enough to hide a person
Skeleton figure from magic shop
Black light and objects as mentioned later, treated to react to the light
Two white and two black cloths (large), two candles, matches

**SCENE:**
Stagehands place the tombstones in front of a black backdrop. The black
    light is placed so as to shine on tombstones.

**ACTION:**
Lights are extinguished.
Two clowns enter, carrying lighted candles. They whisper nervously.
    One starts to whistle.
The other asks, "Why are you whistlin'?"
The first replies, "I always whistle when I go by a graveyard. 'Specially
    one that's haunted."
Candles shake violently. One candle goes out and is illuminated by the
    other, and vice versa.
From behind one of the tombstones an owl's "Who-o-o-o" is heard.
"Wh-at was that?" stutters one.
"You mean, who-o-o was that," retorts the other.
"I'm too scared to go any further," says one clown.
"Me, too." They sit down in front of tombstones, backs to stones.
Clowns talk about ghosts.
A clown in white sheet rises from behind one tombstone and comes up

behind one clown and blows out his candle. Ghost returns.

Same from behind other tombstone.

Clowns flick on black light, and various objects are seen to pass or float in air from one tombstone to the other *(accomplices wearing black cloths)*. The objects are various bones, skull, false teeth which click.

A skeleton appears and performs a dance. This can be a cardboard figure or a dancer clothed in black with bones painted in luminous or ultraviolet paint.

One clown says, "I got a feelin' we're not alone."

Other clown: "Me, too."

Clowns stand up and light candles. In the meantime the ghosts covered by black cloths have come up behind the clowns.

When candles are lit the black cloths are whisked off, revealing white ghosts. Clowns scream and run off.

Lights are turned on, and two pairs of sneakers are on floor in front of tombstones. Clowns return in stocking feet to pick up shoes.

# #133 The Gorilla

## SCENE:

Gorilla — man in rented costume — pacing up and down behind the bars of his cage. A clown enters, fixes his earnest gaze on the gorilla, and recites.

Actually the clown only gesticulates, and opens and closes his mouth as though saying the actual words, which are read offstage and come over a P.A. system.

## Clown:

O mighty ape. Half beast, half man. Thy uncouth shape betrays a plan, the gulf of being at a bound to span. Thou art the link between ourselves and brutes; lifting the lower to a higher plane; thy human face all cavilers refutes who sneer at Darwin as a dreamer vain.

How camest thou beneath this canvas tent? Within this cage? Behind these iron bars? Thou, whose young days in tropic lands were spent with strange companions under foreign stars. Art thou lonely?

What is life to thee thus mewed in prison, innocent of crime? Become a spectacle for crowds to see, and reckless boys to jeer at all the time. Hast thou no feelings such as we possess? Art thou devoid of any sense of shame?

Rise up, O brother, and thy wrongs redress; rise in thy might, and be no longer tame.

*(The clown bows his head, folds his hands, and stands in contemplation as the voice continues:)*

## Clown:

I paused in my apostrophe; *(here the gorilla acts according to the cues in the reading)* the animal arose. He seized the bars that penned him in; my blood in terror froze. He shook the cage from side to side; the frightened people fled *(clowns sitting at a distance)*; then, in a tone of savage wrath *(gorilla parts bars and steps out)*, the horrid monster said:

*(The balance is actually spoken by the gorilla, in calm, matter-of-fact tone:)*

**Gorilla:**
I'm hired by the wake to wear the dirty creature's skin; I came from Tipperary, and my name is Mickey Flynn. *(Lights out.)*

# #134 The Greasy Spoon

**PROPS:**
Sign: THE GREASY SPOON
Trick table (kitchen table with one loose board on a pivot)
Chairs, towel, salt and pepper shakers, sugar bowl, knife, fork, spoon, glass of water with rubber or plastic cap, fly swatter, trick egg, box of matches, egg cup
Waiter's jacket with large pockets

**SCENE:**
Table is to represent a restaurant. Sign is placed. Chairs or stools are set around table.

**ACTION:**
*(Clown customer enters and sits at table. Clown waiter, towel over arm, and wearing jacket, comes in and stands beside customer. Waiter sets table; all the required utensils and dishes are in his jacket pockets, including glass of water and fly swatter. Intermittent attacks on flies.)*

**Waiter:**
What'll it be?

**Customer:**
It'll have to be something light. *(Waiter hands him a box of matches.)* Bring me a cup of tea.

**Waiter:**
Black or green?

**Customer:**
It makes no difference — I'm color-blind.

*(The customer laughs uproariously at his own joke. He slaps the loose board vigorously, and the shakers fly through the air, with the waiter making a good catch. When things settle down:)*

**Customer:**
Have you any fresh *farmers'* eggs?

**Waiter:**
No, but we have some fresh *hens'* eggs.

*(This time the waiter laughs, thumps the table, and both scramble for the flying shakers.)*

**Waiter:**
So you want an egg.

*(He produces an egg and egg cup from his pocket and places them in front of the customer. The customer decapitates the egg with his knife and removes a toy-sized turtle — purchasable in most dime stores. Brandishing knife in one hand and turtle in the other, customer chases waiter offstage.)*

# #135 The Great Bank Robbery

**PROPS:**
A large wooden box painted black, with dial in white, to resemble a safe
Two flashlights
Firecracker
Bag of miscellaneous tools

**ACTION:**
*(Stagehands place safe in middle of floor. Lights go out one at a time. Two clowns bearing lighted flashlights enter stealthily on tiptoe. One carries bag of tools. Clowns "sh-h-h" each other. One clown stumbles. More shushing. One drops bag of tools. They run part way to exit. Nothing happens, so they tiptoe back, tripping over tools. They find safe and go around it. They try various tools. Hammer is used. First Clown hits his thumb.)*

**First Clown:**
Ouch. I hit my thumb with the hammer.

**Second Clown:**
Shut up. Just put it in your mouth. *(More tapping.)* Pass the hammer. *(No answer. Repeat. Still no answer.)* Why don't you speak?

**First Clown:**
I couldn't, because I did what you told me.

**Second Clown:**
Did what?

**First Clown:**
Put the hammer in my mouth.

**Second Clown:**
We'll have to use soup.

**First Clown:**
Vegetable or beef?

*(The firecracker is taken from the kit bag and handled with care. It is inserted in a hole in the dial. Fuse is lighted, and clowns scamper to a discreet distance, keeping flashlights focused on safe. Explosion. Smoke pours from safe — powder blown through a funnel by clown inside. Door of safe falls open, and small clown, attired in nightgown and carrying a lighted candle, totters out.)*

**Small Clown:**
Can't a watchman get some sleep?

*(Other clowns stuff him back in box and push all off floor.)*

# #136 Hish-Hash-Hosh

**PROPS:**
A knock-down dining room table
A supported sign above the table: BROKEN CUP CAFE
Large shaker marked: PEPPER
Ketchup bottles and other items as desired
Six loud handkerchiefs
Chef's hat and apron
Tin plate
Insect spray gun with fake needle marked: COLD VACCINE

**SCENE:**
Represents a restaurant. Chef is behind counter. The tin plate rests in middle of counter; black thread leads from the edge of the plate through an eyelet in the sign above, so that plate can be raised or lowered by the chef.

**ACTION:**
All clowns, except one, enter and gather around the counter. One of the customers orders a hamburger.
Chef places hamburger on plate. Customer applies pepper. While he is looking for ketchup, a second clown sprinkles on more pepper. Customer wants mustard, relish, onion, and so on, which gives the other clowns the opportunity to add more pepper when the customer is not looking.
Finally, all sense a sneeze coming on and handkerchiefs are displayed.
Clowns produce the giant sneeze three times, one-third shouting "hish," one-third "hash," and one-third "hosh."
With each sneeze the plate with hamburger goes up and down.
On third sneeze a clown rushes in with flit gun. He sprays everyone, and

they run out.

Clown with gun spies hamburger. He takes one bite and goes through suitable contortions. He sprays hamburger violently and, holding it at arm's length, exits with a final sneeze.

## #137 Hollywood

**PROPS:**
Pitcher of water, banana, chalk, small pail, flatiron, stand, table, bowl of
goldfish containing a piece of carrot, vegetable grater, sheets of paper
Movie camera (box with floodlight and fan to give a flickering effect)

**CHARACTERS:**

| | |
|---|---|
| Camera operator | A Reader or Director |
| Hero | Heroine |
| Maid | Curtain 1 |
| Curtain 2 | Chair (more if desired) |
| Hour 1 | Hour 2 |
| Sun | Darkness |
| Stairs | Shadow 1 |
| Shadow 2 | Clock |

(All characters are marked with large signs.)

**ACTION:**
*(When the play opens, Sun is lying on the stage floor. Curtains stand front, center, back to back. Stairs are at back of stage. Hero is seated at stand on which are the grater and pitcher of water. Goldfish bowl is on the table. Chairs at one side. Darkness stands at other side under a black cloth.)*

**Voice:**
*(Either director's or offstage over P.A.)* Hollywood! A motion picture in
one act, without actors — just characters. Produced by _____,
directed by _____, censored by _____, costumes,
buy low and sell high. Action! Camera!
We find our show has now begun,
The curtains part (1)*, and the clock strikes one (2).
The Sun rises (3), a little bit late,
And our Hero studies before the grate (4).
Over his notes he is studiously pouring (5)
And their contents greedily devouring (6).
He crosses the floor (7), three times, no more,
And a fish in the bowl, also, no more (8).
The Maid comes tearing down the Stairs (9)
And falls into — one of the Chairs (10).

*See **ACTION CUES**.

Our Heroine sweeps (11) into the room,
And the Maid flies out (12) like on a broom.
Seeing a bit of the fish's tail (13),
The Heroine turns a little pale (14).
But now our Hero on bended knee (15)
Appeals to her (16) to married be.
The Hours pass (17) as he presses her hand (18),
But his fruitless appeal we can understand (19).
And so she remains to the end unbending (20),
Which leaves us with no happy ending.
So the Sun goes down, lower — lower (21),
And the Shadows come on, slower — slower (22).
The Clock strikes two (23), and Darkness falls (24),
And, if you please, no curtain calls (25).

## ACTION CUES:
1. Curtains separate and walk offstage.
2. Clock strikes Hero on head.
3. The Sun stands up, rising slowly.
4. Hero stares at food grater.
5. Hero pours water over notes *(sheets of paper)*.
6. Hero tears notes and chews on them.
7. Hero makes three *X* marks on floor with piece of chalk.
8. Hero goes to fish bowl and lifts out piece of carrot which he slides into his mouth.
9. Maid runs in and tears up sign *(STAIRS)*.
10. Maid falls into lap of a Chair.
11. Heroine enters sweeping with a broom.
12. Maid exits making birdlike motions.
13. Hero exposes carrot sticking out of his mouth.
14. Heroine lifts and turns the pail.
15. Hero kneels before Heroine.
16. Hero peels a banana and eats fruit.
17. Hours walk across the stage from opposite directions.
18. Hero presses flatiron to Heroine's hand.
19. Hero places banana skin under the stand.
20. Hero tries to make Heroine bend, but she stands stiffly.
21. Sun goes down, halfway, three-quarters way, all the way.
22. Shadows come on too fast, then slow down.
23. Clock strikes Hero and Heroine, and they collapse.
24. Darkness does a prone fall.
25. Curtains walk to center and assume original positions.

# #138 Human Pretzel

## PROPS:
Barrel

Two artificial legs, stuffed with flexible material (cloths) and matched to clown's costume

**ACTION:**

Action takes place during a gymnastic exhibition or wrestling bout.

Barrel with legs attached to top, hidden by a drape surrounding it, is wheeled or pushed into position.

Clown enters while apparatus is being placed. He climbs into the barrel.

The stagehands accidentally cover the barrel and clown with a mat cover long enough for the clown to stuff the drape inside the barrel and to assume a position which will make it appear as though he were sitting on the barrel with his legs *(the false ones)* dangling in front.

Clown watches gymnasts.

Some invisible black thread attached to feet will enable him to cross and uncross his legs.

Clown gets excited during exercises and unconsciously tries to help performers or contestants.

He grasps his feet and pulls and twists himself into odd shapes.

He gets his feet tied behind his neck and has difficulty escaping.

Other clowns push barrel off floor, the contortionist walking.

# #139 Indian Medicine

**PROPS:**

Typical stand for midway or carnival medicine man

Several bottles, same size and type

Sign over stand: SWAMP ROOT — THE GREAT INDIAN CURE-ALL

**CHARACTERS:**

Indian medicine man in costume

Two clowns: one fat and one thin, both with umbrellas under their clown suits (The open umbrella creates the fat man; closing it makes a thin man.)

**ACTION:**

The medicine man takes his place at his stand and goes into his spiel.

Two clowns gather round to listen.

Every few seconds the medicine man interrupts his long list of cures and says pointedly, "And it makes the thin fat and the fat lean."

Clowns purchase Swamp Root.

They follow one another around the floor, stopping every few steps to sip the cure. Gradually they begin to change in size.

When the umbrellas are half open and half shut, both indicate satisfaction with their figures and either put bottles in their pockets or throw them away.

Their figures continue, however, toward the opposite extreme.

The fat man is now the thin man and the thin man, the fat.

Neither is happy with the result.

They go back and listen to the medicine man's story and again purchase

Swamp Root.

Their figures return to original size and they are quite happy; shaking hands, they go offstage.

Policeman comes in and chases off medicine man.

# #140 Lelani

**PROPS:**

Palm trees, leis, grass skirts

Hawaiian music

Anything to represent a beach: fish net, small pails and shovels

Warm lighting

Sign: NO DANCING ALLOWED

Lawnmower with old-fashioned bulb, auto horn attached

Siren

**CHARACTERS:**

Number of clowns

Clown dressed as Hawaiian dancer

Clown policeman

**ACTION:**

Hawaiian beach scene is set, and clowns and dancer are reclining on the sand. Clowns surround dancer so that he is not too noticeable.

Music is heard.

Dancer rises and begins to undulate.

Pace of dancer and interest of audience quicken.

Clowns clap in rhythm.

Siren is heard offstage.

Policeman wheels in lawnmower, honking horn in pursuit of clowns, who run off. *(Genuine Hawaiian dance could follow.)*

# #141 Liar's Seat

**PROPS:**

A specially constructed chair on an old-fashioned high-backed chair adapted to the purpose of the stunt. Under the canvas seat is a large, deep pan of water. The canvas cover is over a yard long. Fastened to the front of the seat, it is extended through the back of the chair and to the floor. As long as a person stands on this part of the canvas, another may sit in the chair without jackknifing into the pan of water. A plastic ball on a rubber cord is stretched across the extended side supports of the chair so as to be level with the head of a seated person. The standing person pulls back the ball to hit the other on the head.

**ACTION:**
*(Two clowns enter, Clown 1 and Clown 2.)*

**Clown 1:**
I'm an inventor.

**Clown 2:**
You're an inventor?

**Clown 1:**
I'm an inventor.

**Clown 2:**
What did you ever invent? *(Clown 1 motions for chair to be brought in.)* Ho, ho, you call that an invention?

**Clown 1:**
Sure, that's a liar's seat.

**Clown 2:**
What do you mean, a liar's seat?

**Clown 1:**
You mean you don't know about the lie test? Sit down and you'll see how it works.

**Clown 2:**
OK *(sitting down)*. But I don't tell lies. *(Inventor pulls elastic, hitting Clown 2 on head with ball.)*

**Clown 1:**
Tell me, do you know Cleopatra?

**Clown 2:**
Yes, we're very good friends. *(Bing)*

**Clown 1:**
How long is it since you saw the Sphinx?

**Clown 2:**
Why, I was out with her last night. *(Bing)*

**Clown 1:**
They tell me you're a married man.

**Clown 2:**
That's right, and my wife and I have never had an argument. *(Bing. Clown 2 jumps out of chair, rubbing his head.)* Say, how would you like to answer some questions for a while? *(Clown 2 stands on canvas at rear; Clown 1 sits down.)* When you were a little boy did you ever smoke weeds?

**Clown 1:**
No, I was a good boy. *(Since Clown 2 does not know how to operate the*

*machine, nothing happens. Clown 2 looks puzzled but continues.)*

**Clown 2:**
Did you ever drink in your life?

**Clown 1:**
No, I was a good boy.

**Clown 2:**
Did you ever steal a kiss from a girl?

**Clown 1:**
No, I was a good boy.

**Clown 2:**
Did you ever stay out later than your parents said?

**Clown 1:**
No, I was a good boy.

**Clown 2:**
Was your mother ever bothered with wet napkins when you were a baby?

**Clown 1:**
No, I was a good dry baby.

**Clown 2:**
*(Clown 2 steps off canvas and Clown 1 gets dunking.)* Well, what are you going to tell your mother now?

# #142 Magic Handkerchiefs

## PROPS:
Large box covered with black cloth or table draped with large cloth that extends to the floor (In either case, box or table must have a one-inch hole bored through the top center.)
A tray, a water pitcher, and some clear drinking glasses (One glass has no bottom.)
A silk hat
A number of brilliantly colored handkerchiefs or silk scarves

## ACTION:
Table is set up in center of floor.
Magician is introduced.
Magician enters, followed by assistant carrying tray, pitcher and glasses.
Magician bows and speaks in a husky voice.
Assistant pours him a glass of water which he drinks, replacing glass.
Magician takes the special glass from the tray and places it on table, over hole. Assistant is dismissed.
Magician announces that he will cause to appear in the glass any color of

handkerchief named by the audience.

Assistant and other clowns come in and sit around on floor. If no one volunteers a color, they do.

Magician covers glass with his silk hat.

As colors are called — blue, red, and so on — they appear in the glass, thanks to an assistant under the table.

One of the clowns asks for "a white one."

The magician ignores him and requests more colors. Another clown joins the first one in calling, "We want a white one."

Finally all the clowns are shouting, "We want a white one."

This becomes a chant, to the embarrassment of the magician.

The act ends when the assistant under the table pokes out his head and asks in a pleading voice, "Doesn't someone want a yellow one?" This he waves as he repeats the question.

# #143 Main Street

**PROPS:**

A barrel is placed between wheels and has handles attached to resemble a street-cleaning cart.

One push-broom, two pairs of horseshoes

Police whistle, siren

**ACTION:**

A clown street cleaner goes his rounds with cart and broom.

There could be a sign on the barrel: HELP KEEP OUR CITY CLEAN.

Cleaner goes to sidelines, looking for dirt and incidentally to gossip with pretty girls.

Offstage: police whistle, siren.

A small clown comes in on the run. He looks for a hiding place.

Whistles get louder. Clown hides in barrel.

Policeman comes in *(on roller skates).*

Policeman looks for fugitive. When his back is to the barrel, the hiding clown pokes his head up, then ducks down.

Policeman discovers head protruding from barrel. He nods his head knowingly. He signals to the street cleaner and to two clowns in the doorway.

Policeman blows whistle and orders them to clean up the street.

Two clowns come in on trot in lock-step position. They have metal horseshoes fastened to the bottoms of their shoes. *(Comedy horse could be used.)*

Street cleaner is very busy. Each time he throws an imaginary shovelful into the barrel, there are signs of distress from the interior.

Policeman enjoys the scene.

Policeman emits a loud "moo" or uses mechanical device for producing this noise.

Clown in barrel stands up shouting, "I give up. I give up."
Clowns wheel off cart, followed by policeman.

# #144 Man-Eating Fish

**PROPS:**
Large box with one end or side removed; sign: MAN-EATING FISH
The box, inverted, is part of a sedan chair under which a clown sits.
A frozen fish

**ACTION:**
The audience is asked kindly to remain seated during the next act because
  of the danger involved. Never before has the great Man-Eating Fish
  been presented to such a delicate and appetizing audience.
Clowns come in, carrying the sedan chair on their shoulders, with others
  carrying guns, nets, pitchforks, and acting as guards.
The procession circles the floor.
Water spouts through holes in the box.
Considerable thrashing about is evident on the inside of the box.
Guards maintain a discreet distance from the man-eating fish.
The group halts at a spot where a rope with a hook attached to the end is
  lowered from the ceiling.
The hook is slipped under a rope, leather or metal loop on the top of the
  box.
By this means the box is raised, disclosing a clown sitting on a tiny box
  munching on a frozen fish: man eating fish.

*(The following five acts, 145a to 145e, inclusive, might well be
considered instrumental to torture.)*

# #145a Harmonica

A giant harmonica is built up from a board five feet long, 12 inches wide,
  and one inch thick.
A real harmonica is built into the inside center of this case.
Clown harmonicist enters, carrying this large instrument. He seats himself
  on a chair, but cannot manipulate the harmonica because of its size
  and weight.
Two clowns come on to assist him. They work the harmonica like a saw,
  and the player spits out teeth *(white beans).*
He chases assistants away and proceeds to play the harmonica, or if no
  player is available the music can be dubbed in by P.A., providing the
  supposed player is properly placed.

# #145b Harp

A comedy harp is constructed by using car brake pedals, auto lights and rubber or elastic strings.

Harp music is dubbed in, and harp player goes through some crazy antics with the strings, plucking them to ridiculous lengths, getting his head caught between them, and the like.

Player stops to move his harp to a new location, but harp music continues.

# #145c Pianissimo

**PROPS:**
A piano packing box or facsimile
Cap pistol

**ACTION:**
Piano packing box is wheeled into the room. It is made up to look like a piano, with painted keyboard, etc.

Inside the box are three clowns — 1, 2 and 3. There is a large round hole above each clown through which the head may be popped and withdrawn. Clown 4 is the pianist.

Pianist enters with much bowing. He seats himself. Seat is not right height. A book does not make it right, or a sheet of music; but the sheet torn in half is exactly right.

Clown prepares to play. Other clowns have remained unseen.

Another pianist plays "Hail, Hail, the Gang's All Here," as clown pianist fakes action. First stanza, music only. Three more stanzas follow, and clowns sing, with numbers 1, 2 and 3 popping up their heads when singing, as indicated:

**Clown 1:**
Soup!

**Clown 2:**
Soup!

**Clowns 1, 2 & 3:**
We all want soup.

**Clown 4:**
Tip your bowl and drain it. Let your whiskers strain it.

**Clown 3:**
Hark!

**Clown 2:**
Hark!

**Clown 1:**
The funny noise,

**Clown 4:**
Listen to the gurgling, boys. *(He points at box.)*

**Clown 1:**
Meat!

**Clown 2:**
Meat!

**Clowns 1, 2 & 3:**
We all want meat.

**Clown 4:**
Fresh and juicy cow meat, ham and pickled pigs' feet.

**Clown 3:**
Lamb

**Clown 2:**
Chops

**Clown 4:**
Are mighty fine.

**Clowns 1, 2 & 3:**
That's the way we always dine.

**Clown 1:**
Pie!

**Clown 2:**
Pie!

**Clowns 1, 2 & 3:**
We all want pie,

**Clown 4:**
Coconut

**Clown 1:**
And cherry,

**Clown 2:**
Peach

**Clown 3:**
And huckleberry. Mince

**Clown 2:**
Pie

**Clown 1:**
Is mighty fine.

**Clown 4:**
That's the way they used to dine.

On Clown 3's line in the last stanza, the pianist, with his cap pistol, shoots each as he appears. Heads hang grotesquely.
Clown 4 takes bow and exits. Piano is pushed off.

# #145d Saxophone

Huge saxophone is built from sheet metal, with fancy stops and decorations.
Open end of sax is balanced on casters and is wheeled in by clown musician.
The mouthpiece is a kazoo.
Popular music is supplied by band or P.A., and saxophonist joins in, going through some ridiculous movements in order to work the stops.

# #145e Xylophone
# or Pipe Organ

A six-foot plank is placed across the backs of two chairs.
Three or four people wearing large paper tubes for hats, with slits for eyes and mouth, kneel or sit before the plank with their fingers spread on top.
Clown organist or xylophonist enters. Music is dubbed in. If this is to be an organ imitation, the organist plays on the others' spread-out fingers, and still another clown pumps the organ *(slow down music whenever pumper acts tired)*; or, if a xylophone, the artist hits the fingers with xylophone mallets. In either case those kneeling can emit chirps or notes in tune with the music.

# #146 Piano Movers

**PROPS:**
One regulation piano packing crate, ropes, pulleys, chain
A whistle to sound like one from a factory
Small paper-covered book

**ACTION:**
This act should not be listed on the program, but it should occur immediately after the first number.
Piano box has been left on the floor.
A person planted in the crowd stands up and complains that he didn't pay his money to sit behind a piano box. He wants the box removed or his

money back.

Ringmaster says he is sorry. The boss mover is here *(Tony steps forward),* but his men have not shown up. However, if there are a few volunteers there should be little difficulty in getting the piano up in the gallery *(or other section).*

Clowns and other eccentrics volunteer.

Rope is lowered from ceiling. Tony explains piano must be lifted so that rope may go around it. One of the volunteers gets stuck under the piano. Tony stops proceedings while he consults his guidebook.

Tony instructs helper to phone well-known cartage person.

Tony gets under, and volunteer gets out.

Whistle blows for quitting time or someone asks, "Would you men care for a cup of coffee?"

All vanish, leaving Tony under the piano.

Man who first complained comes out of the audience exclaiming, "The way these fellows carry on you'd think they worked for the YMCA." He takes box with one hand and pulls it off the floor.

Note: The success of this act rests with the ability of the performers to give the impression that they are actually handling a heavy piano.

## #147 Professor Bluffo

**PROPS:**

Black curtain

Table with hole in top, draped with large black cloth

Tumbler, pitcher of water

Number of colored silk scarves

Bowl of goldfish

Magician's flower bouquet

Magician's cap and top hat

**SCENE:**

Table is placed in front of black curtain. Tumbler and pitcher are on top of table. Accomplice is hidden under drape of table, and another accomplice is behind curtain.

**ACTION:**

Introduction.

Magician enters in cape, wearing hat.

After acknowledging people on all sides, he removes his hat, and a tumbler is revealed balanced on top of his head.

Tumbler is placed on table, covered with hat.

Tumbler is caused to disappear by shifting hat so that tumbler falls down hole.

Trick is repeated, but before magician can cover hat, the accomplice thrusts a hand up through the hole and removes the glass.

Scarves are waved about and disappear through curtain, thanks to other accomplice. Accomplice's hand waves wildly through the hole in curtain.

Professor Bluffo announces he will turn a glass of water into a man. He raps for glass, and accomplice below returns glass. Glass is filled and Bluffo drinks the water. "And now, ladies and gentlemen, for my next trick, I shall make a bowl of goldfish appear out of thin air."

Magician shows he has nothing up his sleeves.

Accomplice below table, being tired of his position, staggers out, and accidentally pulls off magician's cloak.

Magician turns round, disclosing bowl of goldfish fastened to his belt strap.

Magician walks off angrily. Turning at the exit, he presents himself with a magician's bouquet of flowers *(from any magician shop)* which was hidden in his shirt.

# #148 "Pupburger"

## PROPS:

A hot-dog stand made from an orange crate
Some buns, mustard, signs indicating stand
A rachet attached to stand (makes lots of noise on turning)
A knife
A hot dog

## ACTION:

Clown proprietor sets up shop.

Clown customer enters followed by a dog on a leash.

Business of purchasing a hot dog.

Proprietor cuts open bun, looks in compartments of stand, but finds no hot dog.

When the customer is not looking, his dog is stolen and placed in one of the compartments.

Business of turning the ratchet.

Hot dog is produced from other compartment, placed in bun, and sold.

Customer discovers dog is missing. Big argument.

Proprietor grabs hot dog out of bun, throws it in second compartment.

Turns ratchet furiously, in reverse direction.

Takes dog out of first compartment and gives it to the customer.

Customer and dog walk off.

Proprietor shouts, "Hot dogs, hot dogs — anyone want a pup burger?"

Clown policeman comes in and clears the floor.

*(For any of the following acts, 149a to 149d, inclusive, an announcer tells the story, and the action is pantomimed. The main piece of equipment is a white sheet fastened to a wood frame to look like a motion picture screen. A floodlight behind the screen casts shadows on the screen as the characters walk between screen and light. This is the only light. Other props are mentioned in the acts. Characters must work with their bodies at right angles to the screen.)*

# #149a Hair Tonic

Subject, very bald, wants to grow hair.
Tonic is poured on.
Head is massaged by second party.
A third party, holding a sieve in line with the subject's head, gradually thrusts broom straws up through the holes.
These become more and more obvious each time the masseur stops for a rest.

# #149b Moving Pictures

An announcement is made that the silhouettographs will be followed by moving pictures.
Stagehands cross in front of light, bearing framed pictures.

# #149c The Operation

Patient lies on the table close to the screen.
Appropriate sound effects may be used from behind screen.
Anesthetic — patient is struck on head with hammer.
Many curious objects are taken from patient's stomach after it is sawed open. *(Articles are lifted from rear of table.)*
Patient is sewed up *(large needle and cord)*.

# #149d Patent Medicine

Two patients: one wants to get thin, the other wants to get fat.
Subjects are covered with bed sheets, under which they have umbrellas.
The fat person carries the umbrella open.
They drink from bottles, and by their opening or closing the umbrellas, a transformation takes place.

# #150 Siam Club

**PROPS:**
Framework to hold a door. Sign above: SIAM CLUB
One blown egg

**ACTION:**
Doorway is set up in middle of floor. Clown doorman takes his place at
the door.
Clown members approach, give the password, and enter as follows:
Club member raises right arm and says, "Ohwa."
Doorman gives countersign, raising right arm, "Tagoo."
They bow and say in unison, "Siam."
Member goes through doorway.
This is interrupted by a clown who doesn't know the password.
"But I want to join the Siam Club."
Doorman: "You can't do that until you are initiated."
"Then I want to be initiated."
Doorman signals to other clowns to come out.
Prospective new member is seated on the floor and is told he must flap
his arms like a bird and cackle.
The clown crows.
Members vote, turning thumbs down.
Clown is told that hens do not crow, they cackle.
He is given one more chance.
The cackles are forthcoming.
New member is congratulated and is helped to his feet.
In so doing, the blown egg is slipped into place so that it appears as though
the clown had laid an egg.
Club members all laugh.
The "goat" turns and is angry about the joke played on him.
He picks up egg and with menacing gesture chases one of the others, who
runs toward the audience.
The egg is thrown, the front clown ducks, and the egg sails into the audience.

# #151 Square Heads
# from Round Table

**PROPS:**

| | |
|---|---|
| Two dummy horses | Two jousting poles |
| One horseshoe | Stuffed burlap bag marked OATS |
| Paper flowers | |

**ACTION:**
Ringmaster gives proper introductions.

Trumpet is heard offstage.

The combatants charge in on their mounts.

They have dummy horses built about them, so that all the pacing, rearing and what-not can be done from a walking or standing position.

The riders carry long poles, well-wrapped at the business ends with padding.

The contestants parade the grounds, while lady admirers *(clowns in audience)* throw them roses.

The horses charge each other from opposite ends of the floor. Sometimes the riders clash, other times they miss.

One horse drops a shoe and has to be reshod.

A clown carrying the bag marked OATS, passes between the horses as they charge. They change direction and pursue the oat-carrying clown.

# #152 Through the Looking Glass

**PROPS:**

Full-length mirror frame on support
Frame is same on both sides
Two identical boxes of cigarettes
Two lighters

**ACTION:**

The frame is set up in center of floor.

Two clowns enter from opposite sides and see themselves in the "mirror."

A series of synchronized and well-practiced movements follow as each duplicates the actions of the other:

Adjusting cap or tie

Walking away and coming back

Opening mouth to examine stuck-out tongue

Polishing mirror

Scratching self

Changing expression

Finally, each takes out a cigarette. Places cigarette in mouth. Takes out

lighter, ignites. Reaches through the mirror and lights the other's cigarette.
They exit arm in arm.

## #153 TNT

**PROPS:**
Large wooden box painted black, marked TNT — DANGEROUS, on all
    sides (One end of the box is hinged at the bottom, making a door.)
One lantern
One firecracker
One volleyball
Several lengths of narrow tire tubing tied end to end, and fastened to lacing
    of ball

**ACTION:**
Box is placed in center of floor.
A few lights are flicked off to indicate night.
A clown night watchman comes on, carrying lantern. He spies the TNT.
    He sets lamp at safe distance after making his rounds and falls asleep
    on top of box.
Two clowns up to mischief come in. They discover sleeping watchman
    and what appears to be a fuse *(tubing)* leading from box. *(Tubing leads
    out over top of hinged door.)*
They pull and pull on the tube. Night watchman's business is to hold the
    door shut, which he does with his legs drooping over the edge.
Clowns aren't getting anywhere with ordinary pulling; so as they near the
    exit, they turn their backs on the TNT and put fuse over their shoulders.
In the meantime a third clown has discovered the TNT and the fuse leading
    to the firecracker inside box.
He lights fuse. Firecracker goes off.
Watchman wakes up and jumps up, releasing door.
Volleyball comes booming out, knocking clowns flat.

## #154 Tony's Nerve Tonic

**PROPS:**
A small but specially constructed house: it has no floor, just a few support
    bars; walls are light and hinged so that the entire building can fall apart.
A sign on the house reads: TONY'S NERVE TONIC.
Capitals are in red: TNT.
A hawker's medicine kit with bottles
A bomb (bowling ball)
Revolver and blank cartridge
Slapsticks

Suit of red underwear

**ACTION:**
House is pushed into center of floor with clown medicine-hawker walking inside.
Other clowns gather round.
Hawker opens door and begins his spiel to sell bottles of TNT from his kit.
"TNT knocks out your ailments."
"Give your system a shot of TNT."
One clown buys and treats his pal.
Hawker continues his business elsewhere.
Two clowns gag, get sick.
They get mad and go after the hawker with slapsticks. The hawker seeks refuge inside the house.
Clowns are stumped. They go into a huddle and produce a bomb.
As one clown knocks on the front door, another clown slides the bomb in through a back trapdoor.
There is a moment of suspense *(clowns with fingers in ears)* and the bomb *(revolver — which is inside the house)* goes off.
The walls fall apart. Hawker screams and, attired only in tattered red underwear, runs off carrying his kit. *(The hawker's other clothes meantime were hidden in kit.)*
Clowns chase off hawker.

# #155 Twinkletoes

**PROPS:**
Two men in a "horse" costume. This outfit should have ample material in the middle (pleated cloth on elastic).
A hurdle
Whip
Some colored cloths

**ACTION:**
Announcer: "And now, ladies and gentlemen, we are proud and privileged to present, fresh from his triumph at the _____ Horse Show — Tinkeltoes — a champion among champions. Let's give Twinkletoes a rousing reception."
Twinkletoes gallops in. The front man trips as the horse comes to a stop. Rear man kicks front man.
Twinkletoes bows.
Ringmaster, with whip, asks Twinkletoes to bow lower. The horse bows so low that the Ringmaster has to help it up.
Twinkletoes demonstrates different paces that won it fame. Include the "Russian Prance." Twinkletoes does goose step, then drops to haunches and does typical Russian dance.
Hurdle is placed in middle of floor, and Twinkletoes prepares for the jump.

First effort is a balk.

On the next effort the front man jumps straight up in the air in front of hurdle so that rear man can put his hands under his seat and help him over.

Twinkletoes is now in the predicament of straddling the hurdle. Much excitement as Ringmaster tries to lift rear over. A crack of the whip, and rear jumps into piggy-back on front man and so gets over.

Twinkletoes is now to perform his famous stunt of rolling over. The horse gets down on his hands and knees. The whip is cracked; the front rolls one way, the rear, the other.

Much business of getting Twinkletoes back in shape. Finally, Twinkletoes will distinguish colors.

The colored cloths are held up. Twinkletoes faces them. "Pick out the red one," says the ringmaster.

Twinkletoes can't make up his mind. A girl in a red dress leaves her seat, walking toward the exit.

Twinkletoes prances after her.

## #156 Walking the Plank

### PROPS:
Use a soft wood plank, 14 feet long, 14 inches wide, two inches thick. Exactly in the center of balance, a saucer-shaped hollow is sanded out to fit a man's head.

### ACTION:
This stunt is most appropriate on a stage, but may be effective on a gym floor.

Clown enters from a wing, with the plank balanced on his head. Clown's hands are on his hips.

When he is halfway across the floor or stage, someone from the entrance side shouts, "Hey!"

The clown stops short, grasps the board with his hands, and laboriously turns himself and the board about.

Clown returns to entrance and asks, "What do you want?"

Clown in the wings asks, "Where are you going?"

Clown with board points back over his shoulder and the other says, "OK."

Clown and board turn and start across floor again. At the same middle point the clown at the side shouts, "Hey!"

This time the plank-bearer turns quickly, but only he turns. He begins his return to the entrance when a third clown on the opposite side hollers for him.

The business of calling and turning is repeated a number of times.

Note: The stunt might be repeated with two men carrying the plank, one at each end of the board. Instead of using the sanded hollow in the board, these men might wear skull caps of hard material with a short center spike fitted into a deep grommet sunk in the board.

# #157 What Took You So Long?

**PROPS:**

A clown house is made of 2 x 2's which compose the frame for structure about 8' x 6' and 7' high. One door is provided. Walls and windows are painted on wrapping paper which covers the structure.

Roll of stage money and some playing cards

**ACTION:**

Stagehands place house in center of floor.

Four clowns enter singly and, after glancing about, sneak through the doorway.

The audience soon learns that a game of cards is in progress, judging from the remarks coming from inside the house and from a few playing cards that get tossed over the roof.

Two cops *(tall and short)* discover the game.

They listen in and get wise to what is going on.

The tall cop says, "I'll surround the joint while you go in and break up the game."

The small clown says, "No, I'll surround the house while you go in and break up the game."

They argue, but the tall cop finally pushes small clown through the door.

Noise inside immediately stops.

Tall clown walks round the house and round the house. He becomes impatient and starts to whistle and "yoo-hoo" to his partner.

Small clown eventually emerges and is greeted with a blow over the head from tall cop's billy.

Tall clown, "What took you so long?"

Small clown flashes a roll of bills and says, "Could I help it? I had only two bits to start with." *(Blackout)*

# #158 Wild Animal at Large

**PROPS:**

The wild animal (it could be a bird): adapt any circus animal, such as a horse; or a bird, such as an ostrich, is suitable.

Gun with blanks, salt shaker (large) filled with talcum powder, lasso, bird cage with no bottom

**ACTION:**

Announcement: "Do not panic, ladies and gentlemen, but we have just learned of the escape of a wild and ferocious animal. The ＿＿＿＿

is on the loose, but its keepers are in close pursuit."
Animal or bird rushes in and cavorts around.
There is some delay before the keepers *(clowns)* come tumbling in.
They jam at the entrance, and there is considerable piling up and confusion.
One clown has a gun, another a lasso, another a bird cage, and the fourth, the salt shaker.
Any time the gun is fired the animal jumps or flops but carries on.
The clown with the lasso should be expert enough to rope other clowns by mistake. Whenever this is done the clown with the salt shaker sprinkles powder on their seats.
The clown with the bird cage tries to head the ostrich into the tiny receptacle.
Either the clowns can make a capture and lead the animal off the floor, or the animal can escape through the exit, followed by the clowns.

## #159 Wireless?

**PROPS:**
A number of inflated balloons
A 50-foot length of very thin steel wire, arranged as described in script

**ACTION:**
All the clowns, including one very small one, enter, carrying balloons. All scamper about except the small clown, who has carried in one end of one of the wires to which a snap swivel is attached. The clown snaps the swivel to a ring in a special harness he wears. He stands directly under a pulley over which the wire runs along the ceiling and down the wall to a winch operated by stagehands.
Small clown breaks his balloon and begins to cry.
Ringmaster calls other clowns together and points to unfortunate clown. All clowns give their balloons to the small one. This causes him to be raised to the ceiling.
As he goes up the others show alarm, at the same time backing up as though pulling the clown up.
When small clown is up, the others leave the make-believe wire and gather underneath, trying to construct a ladder or pyramid, but without success.
Finally, small clown throws one balloon away. *(These should be gas-filled so that they stay up.)* He comes down a little *(stagehands operating winch)*. More balloons are discarded, and full descent is completed. Music: "Around the World."

CHAPTER 8

---

# Clown Acts Requiring Gymnastic Equipment

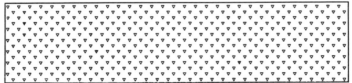

These acts or stunts require training and experience in gymnastics and tumbling. They should not be attempted by anyone without skill and practice. It is a good idea to rehearse them several times in costume, to make sure that the costume does not interfere with the performance of the act.

# #160 Horizontal Bar Stunts

A. Double hip circles:
First clown does back circle to front rest.
Second clown does same exercise part way only, grasping bar inside partner's hands. The second performer's body is between the top clown's legs, and as the second clown circles his legs above the bar, he thrusts a leg under each of the other's armpits.
Clowns are thus locked in position. They start to rock backward and forward until they eventually revolve about the bar. One of the times when they are stopped, the top clown may take a whisk broom out of his hip pocket and dust off the other's pants.
B. Clown makes flying leap for bar. Misses and lands on face.
C. Clown tries to help his pal get up on the bar:
One clown gets down on hands and knees on mat.
Second stands on his back. First clown rises.
Second clown bumps head on bar and falls off.
First clown stands under bar with hands clasped in front as though about to throw the other in a back pitch. The object, however, is to lift him up on the bar. The assist is too vigorous, and second clown vaults over.
Second clown stands on first clown's shoulders, and they march triumphantly toward bar. Upper clown waves to audience, forgetting bar, which hits him about the stomach.
He rolls around it and flies off as other continues march.
First clown gets a stepladder. Business of getting foot through the rungs, sliding down the ladder, teetering ladder until forced to fall to

mat, rolling forward.

Finally, clown stands on top of ladder and gingerly lifts one leg over, then the other, and after much shouting and balancing during which the ladder is removed, clown does a monkey-off. Picks up ladder to exit. Turns, knocking pal down.

D. Miscellaneous horizontal bar stunts:

One clown sits on bar. Second clown grasps his ankles and "skins the cat."

Clown does muscle-grinder *(back circles, with bar across rear shoulders and arms flexed about bar).* Clown does several backward double knee circles, being helped around by second clown's applying a broom to the seat of the first clown's pants.

Two clowns face each other on top of bar. They argue. One slaps the other, who completes a mill circle. Clown One is laughing as Two does circle. Clown Two comes back to starting position and slaps One, who does mill circle, and so on.

Same thing may be done with double knee circles, both facing same direction. Clown One punches Two backward. Clown Two circles bar, and on coming to position extends one arm, striking the other and forcing him backward.

# #161 Parallel Bar Stunts

A. Travels in reverse directions. After regular performers have demonstrated cross-riding seat or bicycle travels forward, a clown runs through the bars lengthwise, and starting at far end, does travel backwards.

B. Master of ceremonies points out the importance of form in gymnastics and suggests that the audience watch for pointed toes and straight legs.

Clown bows. Swings into a handstand and walks the length of the bars with feet pointing in opposite directions. At the halfway marks he stops to scratch one leg with the other foot.

C. One clown swings on his upper arms in center of the bars. On forward swing he rides forward in sliding motion. Backward on rear swing. Another clown at the side of the bars races frantically up and down trying to catch the other. He finally succeeds at the end as performer slides off. Both roll together on ground. One loses his thumb. *(Bends thumb back at joint.)* Business of looking for it and finding it under mat.

D. Clown attempts to walk bars on his feet. He slips and falls between.

Catching one leg on one bar, he circles around it, finally falling on floor.

E. Two clowns do a goose step march the length of the gym, passing on either side of the bars. These clowns reverse direction and return. A third clown, from the side of the bars, does a back circle on far bar to front rest just as the two marching clowns hit that spot. One picks up third clown's feet and the other his shoulders, and they march him off.

F. Clown who is very good at hand balancing walks the bars on his hands. A second clown stands at end of bars, back to performer. Handstander walks off bars onto second clown's shoulders. Second clown turns half about and handstander returns to bars, walking to far end, where he may walk down shoulders of clowns at decreasing height. Final clown may be seated on mat.

G. Two clowns do shoulder rolls from opposite ends of bars, colliding in center and falling between.

H. Repeat above, coming back to back in center in shoulder balance. One clown rolls over forward as the other does a shoulder roll underneath. Come to cross-riding seat. Turn to shake hands and fall off.

I. Clown stands on top of bars. He wiggles his feet farther and farther apart until he does the splits. At same time, another clown tears a piece of canvas. Top clown turns over forward using his hips as pivot against the bars and lands on his fanny on mat.

J. The argument. Two clowns climb up on bars from opposite end, stand up and walk toward center, where they meet. Argument ensues as to who is going to get off. Compromise is reached. One clown gets down with his hands and knees on the bars so that the other can straddle over. The straddler gets partially over and sits down on the other's shoulders. The upper clown hooks his feet under the other's thighs. This puts them in position for a double lever. Top man leans backward, lifting lower man. Teeter-totter.

K. Pinwheel. Clown in center of bars does series of backward rolls from upper-arm hang position. On each revolution another clown connects with a slapstick, thus helping the other around. Performer exits and returns with air cushion attached to his seat.

L. Walking under bars, clown catches his chin on bar and falls to his back on mat. Lifts one leg high as chin appears to catch on bars. Holds arms firmly at hips and beats mat judo style with hands, breaking fall.

M. Clown drops his hat at end of bars. Another clown does a shoulder balance at that end of the bars back toward hat. First clown misses hat. Shouts at second clown to hold it. Walks through bars from far end, passing under shoulder-balancing clown. As he stoops to pick up his hat the clown on the bars starts a backward shoulder roll, and his feet catch the other clown in the pants, causing him to fall on his face.

Clown on bars continues his interrupted swing, and second clown comes back to remonstrate, getting clown's feet in face. Clown exits, spitting out teeth *(white beans)*.

# #162 Ring Stunts
## (Flying Rings)

A. Two clowns sit on floor, facing each other, with rings between them.
   A third clown performs on the rings, with much swinging.
   A fourth clown is called or whistled to, first by one of the clowns on the side, then by the other. This causes the clown to cross in the pathway of the swinging clown.
   The clown who does the crossing over should be oblivious to the performer on the rings, but the act should be practiced so that the misses are very close. The interfering clown could carry a tray of ice cream cones.
   On one cross-over the clown can drop some object such as a handkerchief.
   Next time he pauses in line of flight, but stoops to pick up hanky in nick of time.
   Another time he can slip on the same spot and on his return take out a cloth to polish the floor.
B. Clown does nest hang on rings. Foot goes through and he can't get it out. Other clowns rush to the rescue, take off shoe, tickle bare foot with feather duster.
C. One clown does a back plant or lever. A second puts a towel around his neck and does likewise below the top performer.
D. Two more clowns decide to show up the first two. One does a nest hang.
   The second has a small trapeze with harness attached and with a mouthpiece which he puts in the first clown's mouth. Also inserted at the same time: a pair of false teeth. The under man proceeds to get into position for the act; but on throwing his weight off the floor, the other opens his mouth, losing the false teeth and causing mate to sprawl on the mat.

# #163 Stunt with
## Tumbling Mats

**PROPS:**
Tumbling mats
One 15-foot roll of narrow-width carpet

**CHARACTERS:**
Two clown tumblers

**ACTION:**
Clowns X and Y enter in lock-step position.

Trip on mats and do a forward roll, holding positions. Fall flat with front
man X on bottom. Y is across X in an X position.

X cannot get up because of Y.

Y gets up to a stoop position, and X rises too fast, bumping Y in the stomach.
Both fall flat again.

Y gets to his feet. He picks up X by trouser seat and kicks him into forward
roll. X turns to face Y.

X picks up 15-foot carpet length from side of mats and goes to open it. Holding
one end, he throws the carpet at Y. The carpet strikes Y, who does a
backward roll.

X smooths out carpet and goes back to his position. Y walks forward and
stands on his end of carpet. X gives carpet a jerk and Y lands on his
seat. Y upstarts to his feet.

Both grasp opposite ends of carpet and simultaneously give it a tug. Both
roll forward facing each other. X slaps Y's face *(Y clapping his hands)*;
Y does the same thing to X. X reels half about as Y turns sideways and
assumes a stooping position. X does an assisted back handspring over Y.

Both roll to opposite ends of mats.

A couple of throws follow; in each case, the first attempt is a cropper.

1. Side leg pitch.
2. Pitch back straight leg.
3. Back pitch from shoulders.

X does singles turn down length of mat.

Y takes his turn but gets hold of end of carpet, wrapping himself up in a
series of forward rolls.

A shoulder mount is attempted, but the top man slips off.

His leg gets inside the under man's pants and a funny situation develops.

After they get straightened out, a couple of short, snappy stunts are done
without clowning, and the two go off in lock step.

# #164 Trampoline Stunts

A. Clown steps through cords or springs.
B. Clown faces side of trampoline as though to do back somersault. His
   clown partner runs around to spot him. Clown on trampoline does
   half-twist turn. Business of second clown running to opposite side,
   et cetera. Active clown eventually somersaults off to floor.
C. Instead of rolling into position from floor to mat, the clown gets his
   head caught in cords.
D. Succession of back drops, each one getting lower and lower until clown
   is on mat.
E. Reverse D. Back drops get higher and higher as clown pulls himself
   up on imaginary rope.
F. Two clowns turn a long skipping rope, and third clown skips *(plain
   jumps, cannonballs, jackknives, twists, drops)*.
G. Clown skips rope by doing a series of back drops.

H.  Two clowns facing. Alternate bounces, then one does seat drop with feet spread while other does front drop. To the audience it looks as though a collision is unavoidable.
I.  Alternate high jumping. One clown stops and walks under jumping clown, who spreads his feet. Ground clown walks back as leapfrog is repeated.
J.  Double seat drops. Two clowns do seat drops simultaneously and facing each other. On one bounce one clown sits in other's lap.
K.  Back lay-out somersault to front drop. Performer crawls weakly to side, hangs head over and, holding side bar, dismounts with forward turnover to stand on floor, followed by a prone fall.

# #165 Tumbling Fun in a Laundry

## PROPS:
Heavy clothesline, pegs, miscellaneous clothes
Laundry irons, two cups of water, Thermos bottle
Two medium-size tables, one small
Springboard, mats, two chairs
Clothes basket (no bottom)
Cuspidor, slapstick, broom, four water glasses

## CHARACTERS:
Two eccentric clown tumblers

## SETTING:
Clothesline holding clothes is hung across gym.
On Table 1 are some clothes, cups, bottle and irons. Off to one side is Table 2 with a small one on top.
A couple of chairs stand at back.
The springboard is in line with Table 1.
Sign on table: LO SING & SING HI — FIRST-CLASS LAUNDRY
Tumbling mats surround Table 1.

## ACTION:
Cartwheel entries. Clowns get to opposite sides of Table 1, start ironing. One drinks from Thermos and spits into cuspidor which jumps *(string attached)*.
Business of drinking from cups and mouth-spraying clothes during ironing. When doing so, hold shirts in front of face and once in a while spray over shirt on opposite clown.
This goes on until both get mad. No. 2 chases No. 1. No. 2 runs round table, No. 1 dives over. No. 2 goes round again, No. 1 dives back. No. 2 runs to end of table. No. 1 neck-flips across table. No. 1 hides in basket *(upside down)*. No. 2 continues chase looking for No. 1.
No. 2 gets slapstick and hits No. 1 when he pops his head up. No. 1 does

forward rolls in basket, No. 2 paddling with slapstick. Chase to tops of Tables 2 and 3, leaving slapstick on Table 3. Down to floor and somersaults from springboard over Table 1. No. 1 bounces on end of springboard. No. 2 takes broom and swings at No. 1, who does a backward somersault. No. 2 falls on mat and sits up in a dazed position. No. 1 walks into position for a back pitch.

No. 1 runs and swings forward and backward on clotheslines, smacking No. 2, who is just getting up. No. 1 goes to top table for headstand. No. 2 sneaks underneath on hands and knees and jiggles table. No. 1 hits No. 2 on trousers with slapstick. No. 2 jumps forward, exposing head, which is hit. Repeat. No. 2 pulls a fake and returns to the floor.

No. 2 throws four glasses to No. 1, followed by a chair. Chair is placed on inverted glasses, and No. 1 does a hand balance or one-shoulder balance or chair routine.

No. 2 goes to top table and acts as ground man for two or three hand balances. Both exit with handsprings.

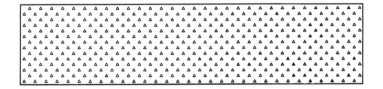

CHAPTER 9

# Clown Acts for
# Water Shows

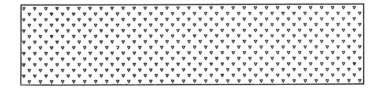

Just as a clown must be skilled in gym, tumbling and trampoline work to perform the stunts in the chapter on "Clown Acts Requiring Gymnastic Equipment," he must be an excellent swimmer and diver to be effective in a water show.

Clown acts in a water show should never compete with or interfere with the other acts or competitive events. They should be used as "fillers" between events, as special acts during intermission, or given their own section of the program.

Make-up and costuming are very important. Also, rely as much as possible on pantomime, except for explanations or descriptions by the master of ceremonies.

# #166 Clown Diving

A routine and script should be followed, and the M.C. should be part of the act, using a P.A. system to inform the audience and for back-talk with divers who should pantomime as much as possible.

**Lookout Dive:**
High vertical jump, one hand shading eyes, one hand on hip, one knee flexed with sole of foot placed against straight knee. Hold position until under water.

**Squirt Dive:**
High jump. Diver hits himself on back of head with one hand at highest point in dive, and a stream of water squirts out of his mouth.

**Big Splash:**
Accentuated swan dive. Hold arch, hitting water in gigantic "belly whopper."

**Standing-Sitting:**
Fanny dive. Diver stands on end of board, does a seat drop onto end of board, then enters water head first.

**Standing-Sitting-Standing:**
As **Standing-Sitting**. From seat drop, diver returns to stand on board, from which position he may do any dive of his choosing.

**Short Board:**
Diver takes running high hurdle and misses end of board, entering water feet first. Surprise — he may perform a half-twist as he passes board.

**Hesitation:**
Diver comes down from his hurdle with rubber legs, collapsing accordion-fashion on the board, finally sprawling into the water.

**Three-Quarter Gainer:**
Similar to big splash. The diver holds his arc, going one-quarter turn too far, to land a "belly whopper."

**Half Jackknife:**
The diver leaps high, grasping one ankle with both hands, the other leg extended backward. Enters head first, maintaining ankle grasp.

**One and a Half:**
Diver does a forward roll on the board followed by a plain dive. When he surfaces, the M.C. asks, "What about the half?" The diver replies, "I did it underwater."

**Dying Duck:**
Divers does a high swan dive. At the height of the dive a blank pistol is fired, and the diver collapses mortally wounded, entering water with a huge splash.

**Partner Dives:**
"Horse and rider" is an example of this type. The first clown jumps high and spreads legs. Second clown, following, dives under spread legs so that first clown appears to be riding the second diver.

**Atomic Dive:**
Diver takes cannonball position *(knees clasped to chest)* in the air and holds it.

**Old Sailor's Dive:**
*(Young sailors know better.)* Diver wears sailor hat. Goes through motions of hitching up trousers. Runs, but instead of hurdling, he hooks one foot behind the other ankle and topples into the water head first with arms at sides.

**Closed Jackknife:**
Diver grasps both ankles but fails to open.

# #167 Clown Swimming

This requires a terrific build-up of a visiting aquatic celebrity *(from Slobovia)*, fanfare, and the like. Swimmer enters in ridiculous costume. Some disrobing may be necessary to get down to an equally ludicrous swimming suit.

The performer will demonstrate some of the strokes native to his country. *(M.C. functions in similar capacity to that required in* **Clown Diving***.)*

## Indian Chief Stroke:
Swimmer wears a feather fastened to band round forehead and says "How" each time he raises right arm in salute.

## Geyser Stroke:
Swimmer progresses on back using inverted flutter kick. Hands are cupped at one side so as to squirt fountains of water into air.

## Double Geyser:
Spout from mouth, too.

## Glamour Stroke:
Back crawl stroke. In the arm recovery, the swimmer strokes his hair into place.

## Alternative:
Swimmer wears lady's old-fashioned bathing cap. In one hand, he carries a mirror, and in the other, a lipstick. It is not important where he smears the lipstick.

## The Egyptian or Nile Stroke:
Swimmer treads water. Elbows and wrists are flexed in typical Cleopatra fashion, and motions are appropriate thereto.

## The Swan:
The swimmer is in gliding side-stroke position, head high. Flutter kick propels body forward, and hands just above the water flap at the wrists in imitation of a bird in flight.

## Local Pond or Stream Stroke:
So called because of the reputation of this body of water for floating debris. Crawl stroke. The swimmer, with his fingertips, daintily plucks offending material from his pathway, disdainfully dropping same out to the side.

## Pygmy:
Racing back stroke. Knees are drawn to chest so that feet are at hips. Feet should show above surface.

# #168 Miscellaneous Water Acts

## Barbershop Quartet:
After a canoe demonstration, leave the canoe inverted. While the audience's

attention is diverted, or in dim light, a quartet swims underwater, coming up under the canoe where there will be sufficient air space. As the singers harmonize *("Swanee River")* the canoe may move slowly toward the shallow end. Quartet may emerge *(in old-fashioned bathing suits, mustaches)* for an encore.

### Doctor in the House:

The announcer asks, "Is there a doctor in the house?" A fake doctor stands up at shallow end. He carries valise. The announcer requests doctor to "come here" for a moment. The doctor steps into shallow water and walks length of pool underwater, very unconcerned. *(The valise is filled with weights.)*

### Monte Carlo Sack Stunt:

An escape artist *(?)* is tied inside a sack and thrown into the water. Seconds later he appears, carrying the bag in one hand. The secret: an accomplice and a second sack are required. One sack is inside the other. The artist gets inside the outer sack, but it is the protruding neck of the inside sack that is tied with cord. The accomplice holds the sacks so that the trick is not exposed to the audience.

### Pole Swat:

Two contestants, equipped with swatters, straddle a smooth pole suspended horizontally over the water. Clowns preferred.

Note: Items in this section are from *Your Swimming Pool — Its Program and Operation*. Published by National Council YMCAs of Canada, 15 Spadina Road, Toronto, Ontario. *(Used by permission.)*

# Skill Classification of Acts

To make it easy to select clown acts by the number of clowns needed, and the degree of skill necessary, the following tables have been prepared.

Classifications of clown acts by *type* (Walk-Ons, etc.) and by *equipment needed*, are covered by the chapter headings and content.

The skill levels indicated below are for *gymnastic or tumbling skills only*, not for acting.

Symbols used at heads of columns are these:

Chapt. — Chapter
Act — Act Number
Beg. — Beginners
Int. — Intermediate
Adv. — Advanced
Phys. — Physical Education Training
M.P. — Minimum of Practice Needed

The acts in Chapter 8, "Clown Acts Requiring Gymnastic Equipment," and Chapter 9, "Clown Acts for Water Shows," are not included in this table. The titles indicate their requirement of special, trained skills.

## Acts for One Clown

| Chapt. | Act | Beg. | Int. | Adv. | Phys. | M.P. |
|--------|-----|------|------|------|-------|------|
| 4 | 3 | — | X | — | — | X |
| | 4 | X | — | — | — | X |
| | 5 | — | X | — | — | X |
| | 6 | X | — | — | — | X |
| | 7 | — | — | X | — | — |
| | 8 | — | X | — | — | X |
| | 10 | — | X | — | — | — |
| | 11 | — | — | X | — | X |
| | 12 | — | X | — | — | X |
| | 15 | X | — | — | — | X |
| | 16 | X | — | — | — | — |
| | 17 | X | — | — | — | X |
| | 18 | — | X | — | — | — |

| Chapt. | Act | Beg. | Int. | Adv. | Phys. | M.P. |
|---|---|---|---|---|---|---|
| 5 | 29 | — | X | — | — | X |
|  | 31 | X | — | — | — | X |
|  | 38 | — | — | X | — | — |
|  | 42 | — | X | — | — | X |
| 6 | 71 | X | — | — | — | X |
|  | 105 | X | — | — | — | X |
|  | 107 | X | — | — | — | X |
| 7 | 124 | — | — | X | — | — |
|  | 138 | — | — | X | — | — |
|  | 145b | X | — | — | — | X |
|  | 145d | X | — | — | — | X |

## Acts for Two Clowns

| Chapt. | Act | Beg. | Int. | Adv. | Phys. | M.P. |
|---|---|---|---|---|---|---|
| 4 | 2 | X | — | — | — | — |
|  | 9 | — | X | — | — | X |
|  | 14 | X | — | — | — | X |
|  | 19 | X | — | — | — | — |
| 5 | 22 | — | — | X | X | — |
|  | 25 | — | — | X | X | — |
|  | 30 | X | — | X | — | X |
|  | 36 | — | X | — | — | X |
|  | 37 | — | X | — | — | X |
|  | 41a | — | — | X | — | — |
|  | 41d | — | — | X | — | — |
| 6 | 45 | — | X | — | — | X |
|  | 46 | — | — | X | X | — |
|  | 47 | — | X | — | — | X |
|  | 53 | — | X | — | — | X |
|  | 54 | X | — | — | — | X |
|  | 55 | — | X | — | — | — |
|  | 56 | X | — | — | — | X |
|  | 57 | X | — | — | — | X |
|  | 58 | — | — | X | — | X |
|  | 62 | — | — | X | — | — |
|  | 65 | — | X | — | — | X |
|  | 66 | X | — | — | — | X |

| Chapt. | Act | Beg. | Int. | Adv. | Phys. | M.P. |
|--------|-----|------|------|------|-------|------|
|        | 67  | X    | —    | —    | —     | X    |
|        | 70  | X    | —    | —    | —     | X    |
|        | 76  | —    | —    | X    | —     | —    |
|        | 77  | —    | —    | X    | —     | —    |
|        | 87  | —    | X    | —    | —     | X    |
|        | 88  | —    | X    | —    | —     | —    |
|        | 90  | X    | —    | —    | —     | X    |
|        | 100 | X    | —    | —    | —     | X    |
|        | 108 | X    | —    | —    | —     | X    |
|        | 110 | X    | —    | —    | —     | X    |
|        | 112 | —    | X    | —    | —     | X    |
|        | 113 | X    | —    | —    | —     | X    |
| 7      | 116 | —    | —    | X    | —     | —    |
|        | 120 | —    | X    | —    | —     | X    |
|        | 131 | —    | X    | —    | —     | X    |
|        | 133 | —    | X    | —    | —     | X    |
|        | 134 | —    | X    | —    | —     | —    |
|        | 141 | —    | —    | X    | —     | —    |
|        | 142 | —    | X    | —    | —     | X    |
|        | 147 | —    | —    | X    | —     | —    |
|        | 152 | —    | —    | X    | —     | —    |
|        | 155 | —    | X    | —    | —     | —    |

## Acts for Three to Five Clowns

| Chapt. | Act | Beg. | Int. | Adv. | Phys. | M.P. |
|--------|-----|------|------|------|-------|------|
| 4      | 20  | X    | —    | —    | —     | —    |
| 5      | 23  | —    | X    | —    | —     | —    |
|        | 24  | X    | —    | —    | —     | X    |
|        | 28  | X    | —    | —    | —     | X    |
|        | 34  | X    | —    | —    | —     | X    |
|        | 35  | X    | —    | —    | —     | X    |
|        | 41b | —    | —    | X    | —     | —    |
|        | 41c | —    | —    | X    | —     | —    |
|        | 41e | —    | —    | X    | —     | —    |
|        | 41f | —    | —    | X    | —     | —    |
|        | 43  | —    | —    | X    | —     | X    |
| 6      | 50  | —    | X    | —    | —     | X    |
|        | 51  | X    | —    | —    | —     | X    |
|        | 59  | X    | —    | —    | X     | X    |
|        | 60  | —    | —    | X    | —     | —    |

| Chapt. | Act | Beg. | Int. | Adv. | Phys. | M.P. |
|---|---|---|---|---|---|---|
| | 68 | X | — | — | — | X |
| | 69 | — | — | X | — | — |
| | 72 | — | X | — | — | — |
| | 74 | — | X | — | — | X |
| | 75 | X | — | — | — | X |
| | 79 | — | — | X | — | X |
| | 80 | — | X | — | — | X |
| | 81 | — | — | X | — | — |
| | 82 | X | — | — | — | X |
| | 84 | — | — | X | — | — |
| | 85 | — | — | X | — | — |
| | 86 | — | X | — | — | X |
| | 89 | — | X | — | X | — |
| | 93 | — | X | — | — | X |
| | 95 | — | — | X | — | X |
| | 101 | X | — | — | — | — |
| | 102 | — | X | — | — | — |
| | 103 | X | — | — | X | X |
| | 109 | — | — | X | — | — |
| | 111 | — | X | — | — | — |
| | 114 | — | X | — | — | X |
| 7 | 115 | — | X | — | — | X |
| | 117 | — | X | — | — | — |
| | 118 | X | — | — | — | X |
| | 119 | — | — | X | — | — |
| | 121 | — | X | — | — | — |
| | 123 | — | — | X | — | — |
| | 125 | X | — | — | — | X |
| | 126 | X | — | — | — | X |
| | 128 | — | X | — | X | X |
| | 132 | — | X | — | — | — |
| | 135 | — | X | — | — | — |
| | 139 | X | — | — | — | — |
| | 143 | X | — | — | — | X |
| | 145a | — | — | X | — | X |
| | 145c | — | — | X | — | — |
| | 145e | — | — | X | — | — |
| | 148 | X | — | — | — | X |
| | 149 | X | — | — | — | — |
| | 153 | X | — | — | — | X |
| | 156 | X | — | — | — | X |

# Acts for Six or More Clowns

| Chapt. | Act | Beg. | Int. | Adv. | Phys. | M.P. |
|--------|-----|------|------|------|-------|------|
| 5 | 21 | X | — | — | — | X |
|  | 26 | — | — | X | — | — |
|  | 27 | — | X | — | — | X |
|  | 32 | X | — | — | — | X |
|  | 39 | X | — | — | — | X |
|  | 40 | — | — | X | — | X |
| 6 | 48 | X | — | — | — | X |
|  | 49 | — | — | X | — | — |
|  | 52 | — | X | — | — | X |
|  | 61 | — | — | X | — | — |
|  | 63 | — | X | — | X | — |
|  | 64 | X | — | — | — | X |
|  | 73 | X | — | — | — | — |
|  | 78 | — | X | — | X | — |
|  | 83 | X | — | — | X | X |
|  | 91 | X | — | — | — | — |
|  | 92 | — | X | — | — | — |
|  | 94 | X | — | — | — | — |
|  | 96 | — | X | — | — | X |
|  | 97 | — | — | X | — | — |
|  | 98 | X | — | — | X | — |
|  | 99 | X | — | — | X | — |
|  | 104 | X | — | — | — | X |
|  | 106 | X | — | — | — | X |
| 7 | 122 | X | — | — | — | X |
|  | 127 | X | — | — | — | X |
|  | 129 | X | — | — | — | X |
|  | 130 | — | X | — | — | X |
|  | 136 | X | — | — | — | — |
|  | 137 | X | — | — | — | — |
|  | 140 | X | — | — | — | — |
|  | 144 | X | — | — | — | — |
|  | 146 | — | — | X | — | — |
|  | 150 | X | — | — | — | X |
|  | 151 | X | — | — | — | X |
|  | 154 | — | X | — | — | X |
|  | 157 | X | — | — | — | X |
|  | 158 | X | — | — | — | X |
|  | 159 | X | — | — | — | — |

# Index of Clown Acts
# by Titles

Note: The complete list of acts by title from Chapters 4 to 9 inclusive is given in this index alphabetically, with *number of act*, not page number.

# Resources

**Books:**

Burgess, Hovey. *Circus Techniques.* Brian Dube Inc., New York, rev. ed., 1990.

Feder, Happy Jack. *Clown Skits for Everyone.* Meriwether Publishing Ltd., Colorado Springs, CO, second edition, 1991. Everything you need to know to become a performing clown.

Feder, Happy Jack. *Mime Time.* Meriwether Publishing Ltd., Colorado Springs, CO, second edition, 1992. A "how to" manual for beginning mimes with make-up, prop and staging techniques.

Fife, Bruce, et al. *Creative Clowning.* Piccadilly Books, Colorado Springs, CO, second edition, 1992.

Hartisch, Karl, "Whitey." *Introduction to Clowning.* Available from: Clowns of America, P.O. Box 570, Lake Jackson, TX 77566.

Kerns, Ernie. *How to Be a Magic Clown.* 2 vols. Magic, Inc., Chicago, 1960, 1968.

Kipnis, Claude. *The Mime Book.* Meriwether Publishing Ltd., Colorado Springs, CO, second edition, 1988. A comprehensive guide to the art of mime.

Litherland, Janet. *The Clown Ministry Handbook.* Meriwether Publishing Ltd., Colorado Springs, CO, fourth edition, 1989. The first and most comprehensive book on the art of clown ministry.

Litherland, Janet. *Everything New and Who's Who in Clown Ministry.* Meriwether Publishing Ltd., Colorado Springs, CO, 1993. Advanced clown ministry text including seventy-five skits for special days.

Stolzenberg, Mark. *Be a Clown.* Sterling Publishing Co., New York, 1989.

Wiley, Jack. *Basic Circus Skills.* Solipaz Publishing Co., Lodi, CA, third edition, 1990.

**Skits, Plays & Routines:**

Contemporary Drama Service, Box 7710, Colorado Springs, CO 80933.

**Make-up/Costumes/Accessories:**

The Circus Clowns, 3556 Nicollet Ave., Minneapolis, MN 55408. (costumes)

Costumes by Betty, 2181 Edgerton Street, St. Paul, MN 55117.

Funhouse Magic Shop, 6816 Eastern Ave., Baltimore, MD 21224.

Magic Inc., 5082 N. Lincoln Ave., Chicago, IL 60625

Mitzie's Clown Costumes and Gimmicks, P.O. Box 740, Hopkins, MN 55343

Morris Costumes, Inc., 3108 Monroe Road, Charlotte, NC 28205.

One Way Street, Inc., P.O. Box 2398, Littleton, CO 80161.

Pricilla Mooseburger Originals, P.O. Box 700, Maple Lake, MN 55358.

Under the Big Top, P.O. Box 807, Placentia, CA 92670.

**Organizations:**

Clown Camp, University of Wisconsin La Crosse, 1725 State Street, La Crosse, WI 54601.

The Clown Hall of Fame & Research Center, Inc., 114 North Third Street, Delavan, WI 53115.

Clowns of America International, P.O. Box 570, Lake Jackson, TX 77566.

Fellowship of Christian Magicians, Box 385, Connersville, IN 47331.

International Shrine Clown Association, P.O. Box 440, North Reading, MA 01864.

National Clown Arts Council, Inc., 240 Swimming River Road, Colts Neck, NJ 07722.

Phoenix Power & Light Company, Inc., Drawer 5665, Virginia Beach, VA 23455.

Ringling Bros. and Barnum & Bailey Circus, Clown College, P.O. Box 9, Vienna, VA 22183.

World Clown Association, 418 S. Sixth Street, Pekin, IL 61554.

**Periodicals:**

*The New Calliope Magazine.* Clowns of America International, Inc., P.O. Box 570, Lake Jackson, TX 77566-0570.

*Circus Report.* Don Marcks, 525 Oak Street, El Cerrito, CA 94530.

*Clown Alley.* International Shrine Clown Association, P.O. Box 440, North Reading, MA 01864.

*Clowning Around.* World Clown Association, 418 South Sixth Street, Pekin, IL 61554.

*Clown Town Crier.* Clown Hall of Fame & Research Center, Inc., 114 North Third Street, Delavan, WI 53115.

*Laugh-Makers.* 108 Berwyn Ave., Syracuse, NY 13210.

*On One Wheel.* Unicycling Society of America, Inc., P.O. Box 40534, Redford, MI 48240.

*Phoenix Rising.* Phoenix Power & Light Company, Inc., Drawer 5665, Virginia Beach, VA 23455.

*Three Ring News.* Midwest Clown Association, Gene Lee, Editor, 235 South Summit Street, Whitewater, WI 53190.

# ORDER FORM

**MERIWETHER PUBLISHING LTD.**
**P.O. BOX 7710**
**COLORADO SPRINGS, CO 80933**
**TELEPHONE: (719) 594-4422**

*Please send me the following books:*

_____ **Clown Act Omnibus #TT-B118**                    $12.95
by Wes McVicar
*Everything you need to know about clowning*

_____ **Clown Skits for Everyone #TT-B147**              $9.95
by Happy Jack Feder
*A delightful guide to becoming a performing clown*

_____ **The Mime Book #TT-B124**                        $12.95
by Claude Kipnis
*A comprehensive guide to the art of mime*

_____ **Mime Time #TT-B101**                            $10.95
by Happy Jack Feder
*A book of mime routines and performance tips*

_____ **Comedy Improvisation #TT-B175**                 $12.95
by Delton T. Horn
*Improv structures and exercises for young actors*

_____ **Everything New and Who's Who in**
**Clown Ministry #TT-B126**                                 $10.95
by Janet Litherland
*Profiles of clown ministers plus 75 skits for special days*

_____ **The Clown Ministry Handbook #TT-B163**          $10.95
by Janet Litherland
*The first and most complete text on the art of clown ministry*

**These and other fine Meriwether Publishing books are available at
your local bookstore or direct from the publisher. Use the handy
order form on this page.**

NAME: _____

ORGANIZATION NAME: _____

ADDRESS: _____

CITY: _____ STATE: _____ ZIP: _____

PHONE: _____

☐ **Check Enclosed**
☐ **Visa or MasterCard #** _____

*Signature:* _____        Expiration
                                             Date: _____

*(required for Visa/MasterCard orders)*

**COLORADO RESIDENTS:** Please add 3% sales tax.
**SHIPPING:** Include $2.75 for the first book and 50¢ for each additional book ordered.

☐ *Please send me a copy of your complete catalog of books and plays.*